The
Second
coming of
Jesus
Christ

An Analysis of End-Time Bible Prophecy

David L. Toney

WestBow
PRESS
A DIVISION OF THOMAS NELSON
& ZONDERVAN

Copyright © 2014 David L. Toney.

All rights reserved. No part of this book may be used or reproduced by any means, graphic, electronic, or mechanical, including photocopying, recording, taping or by any information storage retrieval system without the written permission of the publisher except in the case of brief quotations embodied in critical articles and reviews.

Unless otherwise noted, all Scripture quotations are taken from the New American Standard Bible.

Scripture taken from the King James Version of the Bible.

Scripture taken from the Amplified Bible, copyright © 1954, 1958, 1962, 1964, 1965, 1987 by The Lockman Foundation. Used by permission.

Scripture quotations taken from the New American Standard Bible®, Copyright © 1960, 1962, 1963, 1968, 1971, 1972, 1973, 1975, 1977, 1995 by The Lockman Foundation. Used by permission. (www.Lockman.org)

Scripture taken from the Holy Bible, NEW INTERNATIONAL VERSION®. Copyright © 1973, 1978, 1984 by Biblica, Inc. All rights reserved worldwide. Used by permission. NEW INTERNATIONAL VERSION® and NIV® are registered trademarks of Biblica, Inc. Use of either trademark for the offering of goods or services requires the prior written consent of Biblica US, Inc.

New English Bible (NEB) Oxford University Press and Cambridge University Press ©1961, 1970

WestBow Press books may be ordered through booksellers or by contacting:

WestBow Press
A Division of Thomas Nelson & Zondervan
1663 Liberty Drive
Bloomington, IN 47403
www.westbowpress.com
1 (866) 928-1240

Because of the dynamic nature of the Internet, any web addresses or links contained in this book may have changed since publication and may no longer be valid. The views expressed in this work are solely those of the author and do not necessarily reflect the views of the publisher, and the publisher hereby disclaims any responsibility for them.

Any people depicted in stock imagery provided by Thinkstock are models, and such images are being used for illustrative purposes only. Certain stock imagery © Thinkstock.

ISBN: 978-1-4908-6631-4 (sc)
ISBN: 978-1-4908-6632-1 (hc)
ISBN: 978-1-4908-6630-7 (e)

Library of Congress Control Number: 2015900541

Printed in the United States of America.

WestBow Press rev. date: 02/04/2015

Contents

Introduction vii
Chapter 1   Evidence That We Are Living in the Latter
            Years.. 1
Chapter 2   The Antichrist 17
Chapter 3   The Ten Kingdoms of the Antichrist 33
Chapter 4   World War III 42
Chapter 5   Judgment from Heaven 53
Chapter 6   The Timing of the Rapture 69
Chapter 7   The Second Coming 79
Chapter 8   North vs. South 84
Chapter 9   The Eagle Has Landed 98
Chapter 10 A Method of Calculating When the Second
            Coming Will Take Place 112
Chapter 11 An Analysis of Daniel's Seventy Weeks of
            Years 119
Chapter 12 America in Bible Prophecy 127
Chapter 13 The Last Seven Years Before the Second Coming
            of Jesus Christ 136
Notes 145

Introduction

Sixteen years ago in 1999, as we approached the turn of the millennium, people throughout the nation became concerned that the world as we knew it would go through some earthshaking change, possibly even the end of the world. Some people feared that the United Nations would assume dictatorial control over our nation in an antichrist-like fashion. Others feared that there would be actual physical changes in the world, including powerful earthquakes and superstorms.

There was concern about "Y2K" effects on all computers throughout the nation. ("Y" stands for *year* and "K" stands for *one thousand*, so "Y2K" stands for the year 2000). Many computer systems nationwide had to be reprogrammed in 1999 so that as we passed into the new millennium these systems would not fail. (At that time, I personally worked on a system in which approximately half the computer programs had to be changed.)

But as we passed into the new millennium, nothing changed. Computer systems continued to work properly (both those that were reprogrammed and those that weren't), our government continued to function as a democracy, and no catastrophes took place. Also, the second coming of Jesus Christ did not take place.

More recently, the Mayan calendar indicated that the end of

this age would take place on December 21, 2012, with possibly profound consequences. But nothing noteworthy happened on that date.

Does this mean that we shouldn't worry about sudden and profound events taking place in our nation and the world? The answer to this question is no. Currently in some Christian literature and on some Christian television programs, Christian ministers who are Bible prophecy adherents are proclaiming that we are currently living in what is known as the "latter years" or "end time," the period of time at the end of this age in which the second coming takes place. I also believe this.

Christian Eschatology

Christian eschatology is the study of end-time events. I believe that these events are summarized as follows, and in the following order:

- the rise of the Antichrist in Europe
- the signing of a seven-year international treaty that allows the Israelis to rebuild their ancient temple on the Temple Mount in Jerusalem
- the desecration of that temple, called the "abomination of desolation," by the Antichrist, three and a half years after the treaty is signed
- the Antichrist's takeover of the entire world
- the demand by the Antichrist that all people throughout the world worship him and accept his mark
- World War III, approximately twenty-one months after the abomination of desolation
- numerous meteors and meteorites, and an asteroid or comet, striking the earth, approximately two years and three months after the abomination of desolation

- the second coming of Christ, the rapture, and the battle of Armageddon—a little over seven years after the signing of the international treaty
- the establishment of Jesus' thousand-year reign from Jerusalem over the entire world, while the Devil is in captivity
- the release of the Devil from his captivity at the end of the thousand-year reign and his leading of a large army to Jerusalem to do battle with the saints, during which fire comes down from heaven and destroys the army
- the final day of judgment, when God decides who will reside on a new earth and in a new city of Jerusalem (which will come down from heaven to exist for eternity) and who will be sentenced to reside in the lake of fire

This book contains an analysis of the numerous prophetic passages of the Christian Bible that concern the latter years. So let's get started on this exciting analysis. In the first chapter, we will begin our study of Christian eschatology by studying evidence that we are living in the latter years.

Chapter 1

Evidence That We Are Living in the Latter Years

There are many prophecies in the Christian Bible that pertain to the last few years, or latter years, before the second coming of Jesus Christ. Some of these prophecies are currently being fulfilled. Thus it seems that we are currently living in the latter years, and the second coming will take place in the near future—that is, at some point in the next few years or decades. In this chapter, I describe how some of these latter-year prophecies are currently being fulfilled.

Return of the Jews to Their Ancient Homeland in the Middle East

This is the strongest indication that we are living in the latter years. There are several passages in the prophetic books (the last third) of the Old Testament that state that because of the sins committed by the people of Israel and Judah, they would be banished by God from their homeland and driven to many other countries. Ezekiel 22:15 (NIV) states, "I will disperse you among the nations and scatter you through the countries; and I will put an end to your uncleanness."

Still other passages indicate that at a future point in time, this dispersion will end, and the dispersed Jews or their descendants will be returned to their homeland. Ezekiel 11:17 (NIV) says, "Therefore say: 'This is what the Sovereign Lord says: I will gather you from the nations and bring you back from the countries where you have been scattered, and I will give you back the land of Israel again.'"

Several passages in the book of Ezekiel indicate that when God has returned the Jews to their homeland, there will be a worldwide awakening to His existence, power, and holiness. Ezekiel 39:27 (NIV) states: "When I have brought them back from the nations and have gathered them from the countries of their enemies, I will show Myself holy through them in the sight of many nations."

See also the following passages in Ezekiel: 28:25; 36:16–38; 37; 38:7–16; and 39:21–28. These passages also suggest that at the time of the Jews' return to their homeland, God will become their God once again as in Ezekiel 39:29 (NIV): "I will no longer hide My face from them, for I will pour out My spirit on the house of Israel, declares the Sovereign Lord."

Many Christian scholars believe that this worldwide recognition of the existence of God will take place at the same time the second coming takes place. This recognition can't take place shortly *before* the second coming, for that is when the evil dictator known as the Antichrist will reign worldwide. He will demand that everyone in the world worship him, and then the great tribulation will follow. Such terrible things cannot happen *after* the recognition of God, because people would recognize the Antichrist for what he is, and nobody would worship him. Also, no countries would participate in World War III, which is to take place just after the reign of the Antichrist and almost two years before the second coming.

Further, this recognition cannot take place sometime

after the second coming, because the second coming itself—a very grand and glorious event witnessed simultaneously by everybody in the world—will cause such recognition to take place. (See Matthew 24:29–31.) When all people throughout the world witness the second coming and recognize it for what it is, they will realize that almighty God Himself exists.

Moreover, after the second coming takes place, Christ will rule over the entire world for one thousand years, after which will be the final judgment when God will determine who goes to heaven and who goes to hell. Therefore, since this worldwide recognition of the existence of God cannot happen either before or after the second coming, it follows that it will happen *at the same time* as the second coming.

The prophecies regarding the dispersion of the Jews throughout the world have, for the most part, already been fulfilled. A study of history reveals that the dispersion has taken place as follows: The northern part of what used to be the kingdom of Israel, consisting of ten tribes, was conquered by Assyria in 721 BC. The Israeli inhabitants were forced to go into exile in Assyria, and very few eventually returned to their homeland. It is not known for certain what happened to them. Because of this, they have been referred to as the ten missing tribes of Israel.

Fanciful theories have come about as to where these missing tribes eventually settled. For example, one theory holds that these ten tribes gave rise to the Anglo-Saxon tribes that settled in England. Another theory holds that the ten tribes gave rise to the Native Americans. However, some scholars believe that all, or at least some, of the inhabitants of these ten tribes settled in central Asia. Wherever they eventually settled, biblical prophecies indicate that they will return to their homeland in the Palestine area and join the other two tribes at the end of this age. Because only a small fraction of the Israelis of the northern ten tribes returned to their homeland, it can be said that the dispersion, or *diaspora*, was already partially under way by the eighth century BC.

In 587 BC, the Babylonian empire conquered the southern part of the former Israeli kingdom (known as Judea), which consisted of the other two tribes. Although most of the Judean inhabitants remained in Judea, much of their leadership was forced to go into exile in Babylonia. However, seventy years later in 516 BC, the Persian empire conquered the Babylonians and subsequently allowed the exiled Jews to move back to Judea. They were also allowed to rebuild Jerusalem and their temple, which had been destroyed during the Babylonian invasion. However, only a small fraction of these exiled Jews returned to their homeland. So a second phase of the dispersion was under way.

A third phase of the dispersion began a few years after Christ's first advent. In AD 66 the Jews in Judea revolted against Roman authority, to which they had been subjected for two centuries. The Romans put down this rebellion in AD 70. In so doing, they besieged Jerusalem, and the temple was destroyed for the second time. In AD 132 the Jews instigated another rebellion. But by AD 135, the Romans reclaimed control over Judea and Samaria and forced all of the Jews who were still alive to leave their homeland and go into exile in other parts of the Roman empire.

The Romans renamed Judea and Samaria Palestine. This remained the name of that part of the Middle East until 1948, when part of it became the modern nation of Israel. So, since AD 135, the dispersed Jews have migrated to many countries throughout the world. Until the twentieth century, no more than a few thousand Jews ever lived in the entire Palestine area.

The prophecies concerning the return of Jews to their homeland are now currently being fulfilled. During the 1860s, there were fewer than ten thousand Jews in all of Palestine. In the late nineteenth century, the so-called Zionist movement began, and throughout the twentieth century and continuing into the twenty-first century, many Jews have migrated to the Palestine area. By 1948, approximately seven hundred thousand Jews had moved back to Palestine.

In 1948, just before the United Nations was about to reestablish the modern nations of Israel and Palestine in the Palestine area, the Jews living in that region took it upon themselves to declare their independence and establish the modern nation-state of Israel. The new nation of Israel currently occupies some, but not all, of the same land that the ancient nation of Israel had before the first advent of Christ. Since 1948, the number of Jews living in modern Israel has increased to approximately six million, which is about 43 percent of all Jews worldwide (as of this writing in 2013).

If it is God's intention to return *all* of the Jews worldwide to the nation of Israel, at the current rate of emigration it may take several more decades for the whole population to return. But if it is God's intention to return only *some* of the Jews to Israel, such a return may be close to completion and may take only a few more years. In either case, it appears that the return of the Jews to their homeland is well under way.

Earlier in this section, I established that the worldwide recognition of the existence of God will happen at the second coming. Above, I established that the return of the Jewish people to their ancient homeland is well under way. Ezekiel 39:27 (quoted earlier) establishes that when the Jewish people return to their homeland, the worldwide recognition of God will take place. Therefore, since the return of the Jewish people to their homeland is well under way, the recognition of God and, thus, the second coming are close at hand. It follows that we are living in the latter years.

The End of the Six-Thousand-Year Period

There is a theory among some fundamentalist Christians who believe biblical prophecy that humankind's existence on earth is to last only seven thousand years. Theoretically, the second coming of Jesus Christ will take place at the end of the first six thousand years. Following the second coming, there will be a one-thousand-year period during which Jesus will reign over all the earth. At the end of this period, there will be a day of judgment, when almighty God will decide who will go to heaven and who will go to hell. (See Revelation 20.)

Many fundamentalist Christians think that God created the universe, the earth, and Adam and Eve at the beginning of the seven-thousand-year period, as described in Genesis, the first book in the Old Testament.

I need to take a moment here to inform the reader of my belief in science. I believe that the universe was created 13.7 billion years ago by the big bang, and that, as scientists profess, the earth was created 4.5 billion years ago, and that mankind evolved from the apes. I don't think that these things happened by chance. I think that God caused these things to happen. If this is true, then some significant event other than the creation of the world may have taken place to mark the beginning of the seven thousand years. For example, maybe Adam and Eve were the first human beings who had souls; or maybe the beginning of the seven-thousand-year period is when civilization came into existence in Mesopotamia.

Some prophecy commentators believe that we are at the

end of the first six thousand years. If this is true, then the second coming is imminent.

The seven-thousand-year period is not specifically mentioned in the Bible. However, there are some verses in the Old and New Testaments that seem to suggest that, in God's eyes, a thousand years is comparable to a single day. For example, 2 Peter 3:8 (NASB) says, "But do not let this one fact escape your notice, beloved, that with the Lord, one day is as a thousand years, and a thousand years as one day." Psalm 90:4 says, "For a thousand years in Thy sight are like yesterday when it passes by, or as a watch in the night."

As discussed in the first section above, several prophecies in the Old Testament state that because of the sins the Israelis committed in the centuries before Christ, they would be exiled from their homeland—and that they would return to their homeland at a later time. Some of these prophecies are in the book of Hosea. In Hosea, God rebuked Israel and Judea for the sins that their people had committed, and He declared that He would punish them for these sins. Hosea 6:1–2 (NASB) indicates that such punishment would last for two days: "Come let us return to the Lord. For He has torn us, but He will heal us; He has wounded us; but He will bandage us. He will revive us after two days; He will raise us up on the third day that we may live before him."

It appears that the comparison of a day to a thousand years applies to this passage also, and that this passage is referring to the destruction of Jerusalem—including the temple in AD 70—as well as the third and final phase of the dispersion of the Jewish people during the last two millennia (since AD 135). Verse 2 indicates that after two thousand years, the nation of Israel was to be restored. Part of this restoration has already taken place, as six million Jews have returned to their homeland, and Israel became a nation again in 1948.

If God's prophecies deal with exact dates, then the third day may begin in either 2070 (2000+70) or 2135 (2000+135). Or it may begin on the day the second coming takes place. But if some of His prophecies deal with approximate dates, then possibly the third day has already started or will begin in the near future. In either case, after reading this prophecy in Hosea, it appears that the third day is the seventh one-thousand-year period and that the second coming is close at hand.

The view that a thousand years can be compared to a day is inherent in the view that the first six thousand years determined for mankind can be compared to the six days that God took to create the world. Christians in the first few centuries after the first advent ascribed to the view that, just as God created all things in six days and rested on the seventh day, so mankind will have an appointed time period of six thousand years and will be governed by Jesus Christ on earth during a seventh thousand-year period.

Apparently, this early Christian view of a seven-thousand-year period has its roots in Judaism. Theologian Grant Jeffrey has done a thorough study of these views of early Christians and Jews. In his book *Armageddon Appointment with Destiny*, Mr. Jeffrey concludes: "Both Jewish and Christian authorities interpret the 'Great Sabbath' as the final seventh day of one thousand years, following the six thousand years (6 X 1,000 years) starting from Adam."[1]

I advise the reader to also read Revelation 20:1–6, which describes the thousand years during which Jesus Christ reigns on earth after His second coming.

Many scholars in centuries past have been of the view that the beginning of the six-thousand-year period was approximately 4000 BC. For example, Bishop James Ussher of the Church of Ireland calculated in AD 1650 that the world had been created in 4004 BC.[2] He did this by calculating when various persons in the Old Testament were born, and when various kings reigned. Using this chronological data, and starting with the birth of Christ, he worked his way backward to the beginning of the Old Testament.

Scripture does not explicitly state that a seven-thousand-year period has been determined for humankind, but the prevalent view in the early church was that there is such a time period. This view should be considered when attempting to calculate when the second coming of Jesus Christ will occur. If the Old Testament is a valid document to use in calculating when the beginning of the six-thousand-year period began, then the resulting answer is approximately 4000 BC. Therefore, the end of the six-thousand-year period and the second coming will occur in some year within a few decades after AD 2000.

Still another indication that we are near the end of the first six thousand years is in chapter 10 of 2 Esdras in the Apocrypha. Verses 45 and 46 state that three thousand years passed before sacrifices were offered in Zion. After the three thousand years, King Solomon built the city of Jerusalem and started offering sacrifices. Presumably, the beginning of this three-thousand-year period is the same as the beginning of the six-thousand-year period.

King Solomon reigned in the tenth century BC. Three thousand years before that was between 3900 BC and 4000 BC. Four thousand years before the first advent of Christ, plus two thousand years after the first advent, adds up to six thousand years. Thus we are closing in on the end of the six thousand years. (Read the chapter titled "A Method for Calculating When the Second Coming Will Occur" to see how I use this information in attempting to compute the exact year when the second coming will occur.)

The End of the Times of the Gentiles

In the New Testament, Jesus said that Jerusalem would be trampled underfoot by the Gentiles until the times of the Gentiles was fulfilled. (See Luke 21:24.) As noted in the first section above, for the last two thousand years (that is, from AD 135 until the twentieth century), very few Jews resided in all of Palestine, including Jerusalem, and Jerusalem was always controlled by Gentile powers. Now there are many Jews living in Jerusalem and throughout Israel, and Jews have control of Jerusalem once again—although Muslims still reside in the eastern part of this city. The old city of Jerusalem currently has Jewish, Muslim, and Christian quarters. Thus, according to Luke 21:24, the fact that Jews inhabit and have control over Jerusalem again may indicate that the end of the times of the Gentiles is close at hand and that the second coming is near.

A Movement to Rebuild the Temple

The return of Jews to Israel throughout the twentieth century and continuing in the twenty-first century makes the rebuilding of the ancient Israeli temple in Jerusalem seem that much closer. Such a rebuilding must take place in order for the latter-year prophecies about this temple to be fulfilled.

There is, in fact, a growing desire in the modern nation of Israel to rebuild their ancient temple. In 1983 a poll conducted among Jews in Israel asked if they would like this temple to be rebuilt. Only 3 percent said yes. The same poll was conducted in 1993, and the "yes" response was 30 percent.

A rebuilt temple would be an exact replica of the temple that was built by King Solomon three thousand years ago, destroyed by the Babylonians, and rebuilt after the Babylonian exile. Currently, private organizations in Israel are making preparations for rebuilding the temple in case the Israeli government decides to embark upon such a project. Many of the implements (vessels) used in the ancient temple worship have already been made, and young men are currently being trained to be priests in the rebuilt temple.

The location of the rebuilt temple would be exactly where it existed previously—on a raised area called the Temple Mount in the eastern part of the old city of Jerusalem. Some scholars believe that this temple was located at the center of the Temple Mount, but a few believe that it was on the northern part. If it was in the center, then the Muslim holy shrine known as the Dome of the Rock (the site where Mohammed theoretically ascended into heaven), which is in the center of the Temple Mount, would first have to be torn down to make room for the temple. It is hard to see how Muslims throughout the Middle East would stand for such an action. If hard evidence can be found that proves that the temple was in the northern part, then there would be enough room to build it there again, along with an altar and other structures used in temple worship. There would be space to spare, and the Dome of the Rock would not be disturbed. Revelation 11:1–2 refers to the temple that will exist in the latter years (the one that has yet to be built) and seems to suggest a possible coexistence of these two holy buildings.

Wherever the new temple will be built on the Temple Mount, since many Jews are back in their homeland and control Jerusalem, the rebuilding of the temple seems more likely than in previous centuries, and the latter-year prophecies concerning the temple, followed by the second coming, may soon come to pass.

Preaching of the Gospel throughout the Whole World

Matthew 24:14 (NASB) states: "And this gospel of the kingdom shall be preached in the whole world for a witness to all the nations, and then the end shall come."

Throughout the last two thousand years, the Word of the Lord has been spread throughout the world. So it now seems likely that we are approaching that point in time when all the peoples of the world have finally heard the Word of the Lord. If not all peoples of the world have heard the Word, then surely almost all peoples have. Thus we are approaching that point in time when the end shall come and the second coming will take place.

It should be noted that the preaching of the gospel to people who have not yet heard it for the first time took place even as late as the twentieth century. For example, it wasn't until the 1930s that the white man penetrated into and explored the interior of the large island of New Guinea, northeast of Australia. Probably the native tribes in the interior of New Guinea had not heard the Word of the Lord until such exploration took place. Likewise, the spreading of the gospel for the first time among some Indian tribes in South America was continuing at least as late as the 1950s.

Since the spreading of the gospel to all peoples is now completed, or nearly completed, "the end will come" in the not-too-distant future, and the second coming will then take place. Note that Matthew 24:14, quoted above, does not indicate that all people who have heard the Word of the Lord—or even most of them—will be saved. It only states that all peoples will hear the message. Thus, even though the majority of the world's population is still unsaved, the end of this age may be near.

The Spread of Nuclear Weapons

There are three passages in the Bible that seem to suggest that nuclear weapons will be used during World War III (WWIII).

"This is the plague with which the Lord will strike all the nations that fought against Jerusalem: Their flesh will rot while they are still standing on their feet, their eyes will rot in their sockets, and their tongues will rot in their mouths" (Zech. 14:12 NIV).

Their flesh rotting while they are standing on their feet must refer to the effects of a nearby nuclear explosion. The bodies are burned up instantly before they have a chance to fall to the ground.

"The two that survived will be destroyed by the sword; one of them will fall by the sword of the other, who will himself fall by the sword in the last days" (2 Esd. 12:28 NEB).

As I discuss in the chapter titled "The Eagle Has Landed," this passage refers to Russia being destroyed by the United States, which in turn is also defeated by military action. It is hard to see the United States defeating Russia by conventional weapons alone. Therefore, the United States will use nuclear weapons to defeat Russia. Possibly the United States will strike Russia with a preemptive first strike. Also, Russia will send nuclear missiles to the United States, but this bombardment won't be as severe as the US attack on Russia. So the United States will exist for a while longer before it succumbs to the Russian attack.

Revelation 9:13–19 discusses the fact that one third of the world's population is going to die from military action. Conventional warfare is not severe enough to kill one third of the world's population. Worldwide nuclear warfare will evidently take place.

Verses that indicate that nuclear warfare will take place don't necessarily indicate that it will take place in the *near future*. They only indicate that it will happen sometime in the future. But the fact that it can happen in the near future is demonstrated by the fact that eight countries, so far, have nuclear weapons and the missiles to deliver them: the United States, Russia, Britain, France, China, India, Pakistan, and Israel. Read the chapter titled "World War III" for further discussion.

It should be noted that many passages in the Bible state that in the latter years there will be widespread destruction from fire. Read 2 Peter 3:10–12 for an example of this. Some commentators believe that such passages refer to nuclear warfare. However, that is not what I believe. I am of the opinion that such passages refer to the effects of billions of meteors and meteorites, and an asteroid or comet, speeding down through the earth's atmosphere, which will happen during the great tribulation. (See the chapter titled "Judgment from Heaven.")

The Unification of Europe

Bible prophecies indicate that shortly before the second coming, there will be an evil dictator known as the Antichrist, who will rise to power in Europe and subject the entire world to his authority. Currently, Europe appears to be in the process of becoming a united confederation of nation-states under the auspices of the organization called the European Union (formerly called the Common Market and the European Community). If this current trend of increased unification among European countries continues, it may be setting the stage for the Antichrist to come to power. Europe may become a large democracy with a federal government stronger than the national governments of its individual nations—in a manner similar to the United States.

The Antichrist may start out as a high-ranking official,

either a political appointee or an elected official in the democratic European Union government. He would then only have to acquire more power thru political intrigue until he acquired complete control over the EU, thus changing it from a democracy to a dictatorship—in a manner similar to the way Adolph Hitler gained absolute power in Germany in the 1930s. The current gradual unification of Europe through the strengthening of the EU makes it seem plausible that the rise of the Antichrist, which will be followed a few years later by the second coming of Jesus, could take place in the near future.

The Rise of Russia

Ezekiel 38 and 39 and Daniel 11:40–45 indicate that Russia and her allies will invade the Middle East just before the end of this age, after the Jews have returned to their homeland and just before the second coming. Not until the years following World War II has Russia had the military might and aggressiveness to mount such an extensive invasion. It now seems plausible that Russia might mount such an invasion in the next few years or decades following the reign of the Antichrist, and that the prophecies in Ezekiel 38 and 39 and Daniel 11:40–45 are about to be fulfilled.

Note that this increased aggressiveness and military might on the part of Russia doesn't necessarily mean that Russia *will* mount such an invasion in the near future. It only means that it *can* mount such an invasion. In other words, Russia must have military might and aggressiveness before it can mount such an invasion. It now has these two attributes, so an invasion in the near future seems plausible.

Modern Communications Technology

Consider the manner in which the two witnesses are described in Revelation 11. Verse 9 indicates that the whole world will be watching them as they lie dead for three and a half days and then are resurrected. Although this period of time is only three and a half days, the whole world rejoices over their deaths. How could the whole world find out about their deaths in only three and a half days in order to rejoice over them if it weren't for modern, twenty-first-century communications technology to transmit instantaneously the news of their deaths?

We are living in a time when these two witnesses can be viewed by the whole world on television, and their prophesying, deaths, and resurrections can be viewed as they happen by people throughout the world. So it is now possible for this Revelation prophecy about the whole world viewing these two witnesses to come true. Note that the world's possession of this modern communications technology doesn't necessarily indicate that the two witnesses' prophesying *will* take place in the near future. It only indicates that it *can* take place in the near future, followed within a few months or a few years by the second coming of Christ.

Putting It All-together

If only one of the phenomena described in this chapter was currently taking place, it might not seem like strong evidence that we are living in the latter years. But *all* of the events or phenomena described herein are currently taking place at the same time. That makes it seem like strong evidence that we are living in the latter years and that the second coming of Christ is near.

Chapter 2

The Antichrist

Definition of the Antichrist

According to Bible prophecy, in the latter years shortly before the second coming of Jesus Christ, there will arise an evil dictator who will acquire control over the entire world. This person is commonly referred to as the Antichrist.

Actually, the terms *antichrist* and *antichrists* are used only in 1 John and 2 John in the New Testament. *Antichrist* is used in 1 John 2:18, 22; 4:3; and 2 John 7. *Antichrists* is used in 1 John 2:18. In these passages, the *antichrist* is used to refer to anybody who does not believe that Jesus Christ, in His first appearance on earth, was the incarnate Son of God.

However, passages in the book of Daniel in the Old Testament and in 2 Thessalonians and Revelation in the New Testament describe an evil world dictator who is to reign for a few short years immediately prior to the second coming of Christ. These descriptions are similar enough to suggest that they refer to the same person. For example, both Daniel and Revelation contain passages that state that the Antichrist will have control over ten kingdoms. (See Daniel 7:7–8, 24; and Revelation 17:12–13.)

Also, both Daniel and Revelation state that this person will have authority to do whatever he wants to do for three and a half years. (See Daniel 7:25 and Revelation 13:5.) Take note that in the book of Daniel, the word *time* is often used in place of "year." So *time* means "year," *times* means "two years," and *half a time* means "half a year." So, "a time, times, and half a time" (NASB) add up to three and a half years.

A third similarity between the passages in Revelation 19:19–20 and 2 Thessalonians 2:8 is the indication that the Antichrist will be slain when the second coming takes place. A fourth similarity indicates that this latter-year dictator will be an evil person. (See Daniel 7:8, 11, 20–21, 25; Revelation 13:2–7; and 2 Thessalonians 2:3–4, 9). A fifth similarity of the passages indicates that the activities of the Antichrist will be in accord with the activities of Satan (2 Thes. 2:9; Rev. 13:4).

Although Daniel 7:25 and Revelation 13:5 say that the Antichrist will have authority to do whatever he wants for three and a half years, his whole career will last longer than that. As will be brought out in the chapter titled "An Analysis of Daniel's Seventy Weeks of Years," the Antichrist will sign a seven-year treaty about seven years before the second coming takes place. At that point, he will probably be the leader of the European Union (EU) but not yet dictator of the whole world. The seven-year duration of the treaty plus his time as a politician or political appointee before signing the treaty could add up to a fairly long career. Probably, as of the writing of this chapter (in 2013), the first several years of the Antichrist's career have already passed.

In later chapters of this book, I refer several times to the "reign of the Antichrist." By this I mean the three-and-a-half-year period during which the Antichrist will be free to do whatever he wants to do, not his entire career.

Christians won't be able to identify who the Antichrist is until he acquires dictatorial control over Europe.

Daniel's Chapter 2

In two chapters of the book of Daniel are two separate passages that discuss four empires.

The first passage is in Daniel 2. In this passage, Nebuchadnezzar, the king of Babylon during the Babylonian exile of the Hebrews, had a dream for which he wanted an interpretation. In fact, he wanted not only an interpretation of the dream, but he wanted someone to tell him what the dream was in the first place.

The king sent for the Babylonian magicians and sorcerers, but they said they would only provide an interpretation of the dream after the king described the dream to them. Enraged, Nebuchadnezzar vowed to have all of the wise men of Babylon slain. When the prophet Daniel, one of the Hebrew wise men during the Babylonian exile, found out about this death threat, he asked if the king would give him time to prepare an interpretation of the dream. Daniel was granted this request, and later during a night vision, God related to Daniel what the dream was and its interpretation.

The dream was about a large, magnificent statue. It had a head made of gold; its breast and arms were made of silver; its belly and thighs were made of bronze; its legs were made of iron, and its feet were part iron and part clay. A cut stone struck the feet of the statue and crushed them. Then the stone crushed the entire statue, which became like chaff that was carried away by the wind so that not a trace of the statue was left. The stone that struck the statue became a great mountain.

According to Daniel's interpretation of the dream, Nebuchadnezzar was the head of gold. After his reign, there would be a second kingdom that corresponded to the breast and arms of silver. Then there would be a third kingdom of bronze. After that, there would be a fourth kingdom, as strong as iron. However, inasmuch as the feet and toes were made of iron and clay, this kingdom would be a divided kingdom, part of it strong and part of it brittle. Then almighty God would create another kingdom, which would crush these four kingdoms. This last kingdom would exist forever.

A study of history reveals that the second, third, and fourth kingdoms have come into existence. The Media-Persian empire, which corresponds to the two arms of silver, arose and conquered the Babylonian empire in the sixth century BC. The Greek empire, headed by Alexander the Great in the fourth century BC, conquered the Media-Persian empire. Then a fourth empire arose. Most prophecy commentators say that it was the Roman empire. The identity of the fourth empire will be discussed in the next chapter.

The Antichrist is not discussed in Daniel 2, but we see in the following text that he will arise within this fourth empire.

Daniel's Chapter 7

The second passage about the four empires is in Daniel 7. A few years after Daniel interpreted the dream about the statue for Nebuchadnezzar, Daniel had another dream about four empires. In this dream, the four empires were portrayed as four beasts coming up from the sea. The first one was like a lion with the wings of an eagle. The second beast resembled a bear. The third one was like a leopard with four wings and four heads. The fourth beast was exceptional.

> After this I kept looking in the night visions, and behold, a fourth beast, dreadful and terrifying and extremely strong; and it had iron teeth. It

devoured and crushed, and trampled down the remainder with its feet; and it was different from all the beasts that were before it, and it had ten horns. While I was contemplating the horns, behold, another horn, a little one, came up among them, and three of the first horns were pulled out by the roots before it; and behold, this horn possessed eyes like the eyes of a man, and a mouth uttering great boasts. (Daniel 7:7–8 NASB)

Verses 11 and 12 state that the four beasts will be done away with. (See the last section of the chapter titled "Judgment from Heaven" for an analysis of verses 11 and 12.) After this, per verses 13 and 14, the Son of God is given dominion over all the earth.

In verse 16, Daniel, in his dream, asked a nearby bystander for an interpretation of everything he had seen. According to the bystander, the four beasts stood for four kings who would rise to power, but the saints of the highest one (God) would receive the kingdom and possess it forever.

Verse 23 gives us more information about the fourth beast. "Thus he said: 'The fourth beast will be a fourth kingdom on the earth, which will be different from all the other kingdoms, and it will devour the whole earth and tread it down and crush it'" (Dan. 7:23 NASB).

Verse 24 tells us that the ten horns are ten kings who will arise from the fourth kingdom, and that another king will arise who will subdue three of the ten kings. But verse 26 informs us that this king who subdued three of the ten kings will be destroyed. Verse 27 say that all peoples on the earth will then serve and obey the Christ. At this point, Daniel's dream ended.

Most Christian theologians agree that the four empires in chapter seven are the same four empires as those that are described in chapter 2: namely Babylon, Media-Persia, Greece under Alexander, and Rome. It is thought by many prophecy commentators that the king who will subdue three of the ten kings is the Antichrist. If this is true, then whatever the fourth empire is, the Antichrist will arise from within it.

Daniel's Chapter 8

Chapter 8 is another chapter that contains references to the Antichrist. This chapter describes another vision Daniel had. Verses 3 and 4 describe a ram with two horns that butted westward, northward, and southward. Verses 5, 6, and 7 describe a male goat with a conspicuous horn between the eyes, which defeated the ram. After this, the horn between its eyes was broken, and four other horns came up in its place. Then, out of one of those four horns grew a small horn that grew great toward the south, toward the east, and toward Israel. The small horn even magnified itself to be equal to God, and it prohibited the regular sacrifice at the temple in Jerusalem for 2,300 evenings and mornings, i.e., 1,150 twenty-four-hour periods of time.

Then an angel gave Daniel an interpretation of the vision. According to the angel, the vision pertained to the time of the end. The ram with the two horns represented the kings of Media and Persia. The goat represented the kingdom of Greece, and the large horn between the eyes represented the first king. The four horns that grew in place of the large, broken horn represented four kingdoms that would grow out of the kingdom of Greece. In the latter part of Greek rule, another king would arise, represented by the small horn. He would be insolent and would oppose the prince of princes (the Christ) and would prohibit the regular sacrifice.

Unlike chapters 2 and 7, chapter 8 identifies the kingdoms of Media-Persia and Greece. It is widely accepted by Christian theologians that the large horn between the eyes on the goat represents Alexander the Great, the Greek general who, with a small Greek army, conquered the entire Media-Persian empire. Shortly after establishing his empire, Alexander died at the age of thirty-two.

After some political intrigue among the Greeks, Alexander's empire was divided into four smaller empires ruled by four of his former generals. It is believed that these four empires were represented by the four horns that grew in place of the large, broken horn. These four empires were (1) the Ptolemaic empire, which occupied Egypt and Libya, (2) the Seleucid empire, which extended from Asia Minor and Syria to what is now Afghanistan, (3) an Indian empire, which occupied part of what are now India and Afghanistan, and (4) a Macedonian kingdom, which occupied parts of the Balkan Peninsula in southeastern Europe.

There is some disagreement among commentators over the identity of the person represented by the small horn. Some think that this person is Antiochus Epiphanes, a leader of the Seleucid empire who persecuted the Jews and profaned the Israeli temple in Jerusalem in the second century BC. Others, including myself, think that this person is the Antichrist. I believe that the references to the time of the end in verses 17 and 19 are referring to all the time in the future, starting from the time that Daniel had this particular vision and continuing to the second coming of Christ.

Revelation's Chapter 13

While the fourth beast in Daniel 2 and 7 represents an empire within which the Antichrist will arise, the beast described in the first half of Revelation 13 and in Revelation 17 represents the Antichrist himself. Revelation 13:1–2 (NASB) says, "And he [Satan] stood on the sand of the seashore. And I saw a beast coming up out of the sea, having ten horns and seven heads, and on his horns were ten diadems, and on his heads were blasphemous names. And the beast which I saw was like a leopard, and his feet were like those of a bear, and his mouth like the mouth of a lion. And the dragon [Satan] gave him his power and his throne and great authority."

Verses 3 and 4 state that the Antichrist will receive a head wound from which he will recover. The whole world will be amazed at this and will worship both the Antichrist and Satan. Verse 5 states that the Antichrist will have authority to act for forty-two months. Verses 7 and 8 state that the Antichrist will be given control over every ethnic group in the world, and that many unsaved people will worship him. Verse 10 states that some of the saints (saved people) who are alive at that time and who, presumably, won't worship the Antichrist, will be killed, and some will be imprisoned.

Verses 11 through 15 describe the activities of a second beast, who appears to be an assistant to the first beast. One of his major projects appears to be to cause people to create an image of the first beast—an image that has the ability to speak and carry out the death penalty against many people who refuse to worship the first beast (the Antichrist). It is not clear if the activities described in verses 16 and 17 are carried out by the second beast or by the image of the first beast. Nevertheless, according to verses 16 and 17, many unsaved people throughout the world will receive the Antichrist's mark on their right hands or foreheads. Only people who receive this mark will be allowed to buy or sell anything. The mark can be either the name of the first beast or the number of his name.

Back in ancient times, it was customary among some ethnic groups to compute a number that corresponded to a person's name. This was true among both the Israelis and the ancient Greeks. The computation was done by assigning a number to each letter in the ethnic group's alphabet. Then, by adding up the numbers for all the letters in a person's name, one arrived at a total that corresponded to the person's name.

Verse 18 is the only verse in the entire Bible that tells us the number that corresponds to the Antichrist's name: "Here is wisdom. Let him who has understanding calculate the number of the beast, for the number is that of a man; and his number is six hundred and sixty-six" (Rev. 13:18 NASB). Therefore, if an evil world dictator arises in these latter years, and we calculate that the number of his name is 666, we can be pretty sure that that person is the Antichrist.

Although the Antichrist will require that everybody in the world accept his mark, God is very much against it. In fact, God's penalty for accepting the Antichrist's mark is described in Revelation 14: 9–11.

> And another angel, a third one, followed them, saying with a loud voice, "If anyone worships the beast and his image, and receives a mark on his forehead or upon his hand, he also will drink of the wine of the wrath of God, which is mixed in full strength in the cup of His anger; and he will be tormented with fire and brimstone in the presence of the holy angels and in the presence of the Lamb. And the smoke of

their torment goes up forever and ever; and they have no rest day and night, those who worship the beast and his image, and whoever receives the mark of his name." (Revelation 14:9–11 NASB)

This means that Christians will be in a predicament. If they don't accept the mark, they won't be able to buy food and other necessities of life, and they may be subject to imprisonment or even death. (See Revelation 13:10.) But if they accept the mark, they will spend eternity in hell—apparently, the lake of fire. We will just have to refuse the mark and keep our faith in God, no matter what happens.

It is possible that a black market could come into existence in many countries throughout the world, a system whereby Christians and other people can buy and sell goods without having received the Antichrist's mark. By taking advantage of such a black market, Christians could continue to buy and sell goods for the short period of time that the Antichrist demands that people take his mark.

Revelation 14:9–11 implies that true Christians will not receive the mark. But this doesn't mean that everybody who refuses the mark is a true Christian. Some people may refuse the mark because they are devout members of religions other than Christianity or because they don't want to become subservient to a dictator. Also, some people who refuse the mark and claim to be Christians may not be true Christians (even though they think they are), because they have never truly repented of their sins and accepted Jesus Christ as their Lord and Savior.

Such a prospect brings to mind Daniel 11:32–35. These verses indicate that after the Antichrist has set up the abomination of desolation in Jerusalem, there will be many Jews who truly have faith in God. There will also be many Jews who don't have such faith but who will join with them in hypocrisy. Apparently there will be many Gentile hypocrites as well.

It is known what number is assigned to each letter in the Greek alphabet and to each letter in the Hebrew alphabet. The numbers assigned are 1, 2, 3, 4, 5, 6, 7, 8, 9, 10, 20, 30, 40, 50, 60, 70, 80, 90, 100, 200, 300, 400, 500, 600, 700, 800, and 900. If the Antichrist turns out to have a non-Hebrew name, then his name will have to be translated into Hebrew in order to calculate a number that corresponds to his name using the Hebrew alphabet. Likewise, if the Antichrist has a non-Greek name, then his name will have to be made into a Greek name before calculating his number using the Greek alphabet.

Many teachers of prophecy hold the view that the mark each person receives under the rule of the Antichrist will be a bit of data specific to that person, such as his or her name, birth date, Social Security number, and so on. Some commentators have pointed out that it is now possible to put computer chips underneath the skin, which contain identifying information. This is currently being done for some pets. If a "marked" pet gets lost, employees of animal rescue shelters can wave a wand over the computer chip and read the identifying data of the pet's owner.

However, the Bible does not state or imply that the identifying information a person receives is about that individual. Rather, verse 17 specifically states that the mark a person receives is either the name of the Antichrist or the number of the Antichrist's name. And it may be something as simple as a tattoo, rather than a computer chip.

Since verse 17 states that no one will be able to buy or sell anything unless he has the mark, then any potential customer at any store in the world will be required to have a mark that is visible to the sales person. Also, the sales person will have to have a mark that is visible to the customer.

The question arises: how will financial transactions be handled when the buyer and seller don't see each other face-to-face and neither can verify that the other has accepted the mark? For example, what about cases where someone calls an 800 number to make a purchase over the telephone? What about the payment of bills by personal checks sent through the US mail or purchases made over the Internet. How can it be verified that users of eBay, Craigslist, and Amazon.com have accepted the mark? What about the thousands of financial transactions completed every day over the Internet where companies' stocks are bought and sold automatically by computers?

One solution to these problems could be the creation of national, computerized databases in all countries throughout the world. Each database would contain identifying data on people involved in performing financial transactions where the buyer and seller cannot see each other face-to-face. The databases would contain such data only for persons who have received the mark. Anybody who has received the mark and anticipates being involved in any way in such financial transactions would be required to first visit a government office. A clerk there would verify that the person has the mark on his or her forehead or right hand. The clerk would then enter that person's name, birth date, and other identifying information into the database.

Later, when that person performs one of the financial transactions described above, the appropriate software would look up that person in the database. The software would verify that the person is in the database and would then proceed with the transaction. For example, when a person attempts to make a purchase from a company over the telephone, the company clerk who receives the call tries to look up that person in the database using the Internet. If the search is successful—that is, if the person is found in the database—then the purchase is made. If the database search is unsuccessful, then the purchase is canceled.

In a case where a person attempts to pay a bill by sending a personal check through the US mail, a clerk who receives the check attempts to look up that person in the database. If the search is successful, then the check is accepted and the bill is paid. If the search is unsuccessful, then the check is returned to the person and the bill is not paid. In a situation where a purchase is attempted directly over the Internet, the Internet software attempts to look up the potential customer in the database. If the search is successful, the purchase is made. Otherwise, the purchase is canceled.

The Internet software of eBay and Craigslist would be modified to look up both potential buyers and sellers on the database. If the search for both buyer and seller is successful, the purchase is made. In cases where either the buyer or seller is a company, the company employee directly involved with the purchase would be required to have the mark. In cases where a company's computer, not a company employee, is directly involved with making a purchase, perhaps the chief financial officer or some other representative of that company would be required to have the mark. In all cases, if the database search for a person is unsuccessful, then it is assumed that the person does not have the mark, and the financial transaction is canceled.

Setting up such a computerized system would require a monumental effort. The Antichrist will not require anybody to take his mark until he has acquired control over the entire world. This probably won't be accomplished until he is a year or two into his three-and-a-half-year term. This would leave him one and a half to two and a half years to set up the system and use it. Note that the Bible doesn't say that the Antichrist will have control over the whole world for three and a half years. It only says that he will have authority to do whatever he wants for three and a half years. After the three-and-a-half-year time period starts, it will take him some time to acquire control over the world. One and a half to two and a half years is a relatively short period of time to set up such a complicated computerized system. The Antichrist may in fact be unable to set up such a system in the time he is allowed. Or he may accomplish setting up only parts of it.

Revelation's Chapter 17

This chapter contains a rather mysterious description of a harlot sitting on a scarlet beast with seven heads and ten horns. The fact that this beast has seven heads and ten horns reminds us of the first beast in chapter 13, which also has seven heads and ten horns and represents the Antichrist. Thus this beast in chapter 17 also represents the Antichrist. Parts of Revelation 17 indicate this. Verses 12, 13, and 14 state that the ten horns represent ten kings, which, together with the beast, will wage war against the Christ, but they will be defeated by the Christ. This agrees with Revelation 19:19–20, which states that the beast is prepared to do battle with the Christ but is seized and, along with the false prophet (the second beast in chapter 13), is thrown into the lake of fire.

However, other verses in chapter 17 portray this beast as representing a kingdom rather than an individual. Verses 9, 10, and 11 state that the seven heads are representative of seven kings who rule in succession.

Revelation 17:5 (NASB) describes a label that is written on the harlot's forehead. "And upon her forehead a name was written, a mystery, 'BABYLON THE GREAT, THE MOTHER OF HARLOTS AND OF THE ABOMINATIONS OF THE EARTH.'"

After reading this label, one would think that the harlot represents the ancient city of Babylon. However, verse 18 states that the woman is the great city that reigns over the kings of the earth. Revelation was written close to the year AD 100, and at that time Rome was the dominant city of the world, not Babylon. This leads us to suspect that the woman represents Rome. This idea is further supported by verse 9, which states that the seven heads are seven mountains on which the woman sits. It is common knowledge that Rome is the city built on seven hills.

So, how can we explain this apparent discrepancy? The label on the woman's head says "Babylon," yet we have other indications that she represents Rome. One explanation is that the woman represents a sinful, secular, humanistic culture that originated in Babylon and was adopted by Greece, and later by Rome. This culture then spread throughout the Roman Empire and is, in fact, currently spreading throughout the world.

Verse 16 states that the beast and the ten horns hate this harlot and will burn her up with fire. The question arises: why would the beast and the ten horns have such a hatred for her? It's possible that while the harlot represents many different kinds of sin, the beast and the ten horns have the sin of militancy and a desire to participate in the destruction caused by warfare.

2 Thessalonians' Chapter 2

In verse 3 of this chapter, the Antichrist is referred to as the man of lawlessness. In this second epistle of Paul to the Thessalonians, Paul warned them that the day of the Lord would not come until the man of lawlessness was first revealed. This man will oppose every god worshipped, and he will sit in the newly-built Israeli temple in Jerusalem, displaying himself as God.

But according to verse 7, there is an entity who is currently restraining the Antichrist from coming to power. This entity will continue doing so until he (that is, the entity) is taken out of the way. There has been much speculation as to who this entity is. The most logical answer is that he, or it, is either the Holy Spirit or an angel.

This lawless one will come to power, but he will remain in power for only a short time and will lose his life at the time of the second coming. But while the Antichrist is alive, his activities will coincide with the activities of Satan, both of them deceiving the vast majority of people throughout the world with false wonders. While this is going on, God will send upon these people a "deluding influence" so that they will not recognize and believe in the truth. This is done so that everybody who believes what is false and takes part in sinful activity will be judged. (See verse 12.)

Chapter 3

The Ten Kingdoms of the Antichrist

The Origin of the Antichrist

The Bible indicates that the Antichrist will be of European ethnic origin. Daniel 9:26 (NASB) states, "Then after the 62 weeks the Messiah will be cut off and have nothing, and the people of the prince who is to come will destroy the city and the sanctuary. And its end will come with a flood; even to the end there will be war; desolations are determined."

The term *Messiah*, of course, refers to Jesus Christ. The expression *cut off* in the Old Testament means "killed." The word *city* refers to Jerusalem. The term *sanctuary* refers to the Israeli temple in Jerusalem. The prophecy in Daniel 9:26a was completed by AD 70. Thirty-seven years after Jesus Christ was crucified, Roman legions destroyed Jerusalem and the temple within it. Therefore, the term *people* in Daniel 9:26 refers to the people within the Roman military.

The Roman legions included not only Romans but also people from other lands within the Roman empire. In AD 70 those lands included parts of southern and western Europe, Asia Minor, and the southern and eastern coastlands of the Mediterranean Sea. The term *prince* in Daniel 9:26 refers to the

Antichrist. Therefore, since it is the Antichrist's people who destroyed Jerusalem and the temple, then his ethnic origin will be that of people living in one of the lands mentioned above.

Daniel 9:26 does not imply that the Antichrist lived during the time of the old Roman empire but only that he will be descended from the people who destroyed Jerusalem and the temple.

While Daniel 9:26 indicates that the Antichrist will be descended from people living within the Roman empire, Daniel 8:9 (NASB) seems to indicate that Europe, specifically, will be his place of origin. "And out of one of them came forth a rather small horn which grew exceedingly great toward the south, toward the east, and toward the beautiful land."

As I discussed in the previous chapter, the small horn is the Antichrist, who arises from one of the four small empires which Alexander's large empire was divided into. Which one of the four empires he rises from is indicated by the direction from which he is to grow "exceedingly great." He is to grow "exceedingly great toward the south." This indicates that his place of origin will be in the north. Yet he is also to grow exceedingly great toward the east, indicating that he will originate in the west. The small empire that is in the north and west relative to the other three is the Macedonian kingdom, which is in Europe.

The book of Revelation also indicates that the place of origin of the Antichrist will be in Europe. As I discussed earlier, the woman who sits on the beast in Revelation 17 represents the city of Rome. Thus the Antichrist is once again associated with Rome, the Roman empire, and Europe.

The Ten Kings

The ten kings represented by the ten horns described in Daniel 7:7 and the ten horns described in Revelation 17:12–13 will presumably all rule at the same time, rather than in succession. This is indicated by Revelation 17:12 (NASB): "And the ten horns which you saw are ten kings, who have not yet received a kingdom, but they receive authority as kings with the beast for one hour."

The Bible does not state who the ten kings are or which ten kingdoms they will rule. If we are living in the latter years, and the rise of the Antichrist is only a few years away, then the ten kings may turn out to be ten presidents or prime ministers of modern-day countries. Speculation about who these ten kings will be may be fruitless since they are not yet in power. We probably won't know their names until the Antichrist comes to power. However, speculation about which ten countries or regions constitute the ten kingdoms may prove to be more successful. The only thing the Bible states about the location of the ten kingdoms is that they will be contained within Daniel's fourth empire during the reign of the Antichrist.

As I stated earlier, most prophecy scholars believe that the fourth empire in Daniel 7 was the Roman empire. Since the Roman empire (at least the western half of it) died out in the fourth century AD, prophecy teachers theorize that it will be revived a few years before the return of Jesus Christ. They use the term "revived Roman empire" to describe it.

The European Union

The belief that the Antichrist will be of European descent and that we are currently living in the latter years, has led many Bible prophecy enthusiasts to speculate that the Antichrist's ten kingdoms are ten modern-day European countries. Such speculation is encouraged by the fact that Europe appears to be in the process of becoming a unified confederation of nations under the auspices of an organization called the European Union (EU). The goal of this organization, which first came into existence in 1957 as a result of the Treaty of Rome, is the economic and political integration of its member nations.

Years ago, the EU member states agreed that as of January 1, 1993, there would be no trade barriers or tariffs among them. The EU has also come up with a common European currency called the *euro*. Some Europeans feel that unification should go beyond economic and political integration to include a common foreign policy and a common European military.

At its inception in 1957, what was originally called the Common Market had six members: France, West Germany, Italy, Belgium, the Netherlands, and Luxembourg. In 1973 Great Britain, Ireland, and Denmark also became members. After Greece became the tenth member in 1981, speculation that the Antichrist's ten kingdoms were the Common Market nations increased among Bible prophecy enthusiasts. But since then, membership within the Common Market—renamed the European Community, and later renamed the European Union—has grown to twenty-seven nations, seventeen of which are in the euro zone (that is, the seventeen nations that use the euro currency). The inclusion of so many European nations within the European Union make it seem less plausible that the first ten members are the ten kingdoms of the Antichrist. Actually, it would seem prudent for us to consider additional theories about which ten regions of the world constitute the ten kingdoms.

The Fourth Empire Reconsidered

It is interesting to note that there is no indication in the book of Daniel, or elsewhere in the Bible, that Daniel's fourth empire would die out and later be revived at the time of the Antichrist. Yet the Roman empire, among all the empires that existed after the time of Alexander the Great, still seems the most logical choice to be the fourth empire. Daniel 9:26, Revelation 17:9, and Revelation 17:18 all point to Rome.

An alternative theory to the "revived Roman empire" theory is that the fourth empire has not died out but has existed continuously throughout the last two thousand years. In fact, Daniel 7:11–12 seems to indicate that all four of the empires were to exist concurrently. Verse 11 (NASB) refers to the fourth empire. "Then I kept looking because of the sound of the boastful words which the horn was speaking; I kept looking until the beast was slain, and its body was destroyed and given to the burning fire. As for the rest of the beasts, their dominion was taken away, but an extension of life was granted to them for an appointed period of time."

According to my analysis in the last section of the chapter titled "Judgment from Heaven," the phrase "an appointed period of time" actually means a time period of fifteen months. Daniel 7:7, quoted earlier, indicates that the first three empires were to come into existence prior to the fourth empire, and verses 11 and 12 indicate that they will outlast the fourth empire. This seems a little perplexing, since the Babylonian, Media-Persian, and Alexandrian empires all became defunct before the Roman empire came into existence. The Media-Persian forces conquered the Babylonian empire in the sixth century BC, and Alexander in turn conquered the Media-Persian empire in the fourth century BC. The dissolution of Alexander's Greek empire was discussed earlier.

Another confusing factor is the apparent superimposing of these three empires over one another. The land that was contained within Alexander's empire is almost exactly the same land that was contained within the Media-Persian empire, stretching from Greece to India. The land that was included in the Babylonian empire was all contained within Alexander's empire and the Media-Persian empire, including Mesopotamia, Syria, Israel, and Egypt. Perhaps the continued "existence" of these empires is implied by the continuation of a culture of nationalism fostered by them. Ever since the Babylonian empire came into existence in the sixth century BC, that area of the world has been dominated by one or more nations or empires continually.

The fact that the first three empires have apparently existed continuously throughout the duration of the fourth empire suggests that the fourth empire also has existed continuously throughout the last two thousand years. It reached a high point during the time of the Roman empire and has reached additional high points since then, as various European leaders established their own dynasties. Thus the Roman empire is not the fourth empire. Rather, it is the first dynasty within it. The fourth empire is European civilization.

If the fourth empire consists of European civilization, then this fact alone increases the number of possible candidate nations that could be the ten kingdoms. This is because this "European empire" would include not only European countries but also lands that Europeans have conquered and colonized. Such lands include all of North and South America, Australia, New Zealand, South Africa, and the Asian part of Russia.

A Worldwide Dictatorship

The Antichrist will eventually acquire control over the whole earth. "Thus he said: 'The fourth beast will be a fourth kingdom on the earth, which will be different from all the other kingdoms, and it will devour the whole earth, and tread it down and crush it.'" (Daniel 7:23 NASB).

This may seem like a rather damning description of European civilization, but the fact is that Europeans and descendants of Europeans have had an oppressive control over many lands, in addition to Europe, to varying degrees during the last five centuries. (I don't mean to be completely disparaging of European civilization. After all, it is because of European civilization, that Christianity has spread to many parts of the world.) But, it should be noted that there has yet to be a time when Europeans and their descendants have had control over virtually the entire world.

If Daniel 7:23 means that *much* of the world will be included in the fourth empire, then this accomplishment has already taken place (although Europeans relinquished control over some lands to their native inhabitants in the twentieth century.) If, however, Daniel 7:23 means that, literally, the *entire* world will be included, then this has yet to take place. If the entire world is to be included, then it seems likely that it will take place during the reign of the Antichrist. This idea is supported by Revelation 13:7 (NASB): "And it was given to him to make war with the saints and to overcome them; and authority over every tribe and people and tongue and nation was given to him."

Therefore, since the Antichrist will eventually have domination over the entire world, the ten kingdoms could be any ten countries in the world. It may be that the ten kingdoms will be the ten most powerful nations on earth at the time of the Antichrist. Or they may be ten geographic regions whose constituent countries have strong economic, cultural, and/or military ties. Thus it may be that the EU will be one of the ten kingdoms, rather than be comprised of all ten kingdoms. Other possible candidates would include the United States, a Russian confederation comprised of former Soviet republics, China, Japan, India, Australia, South Africa, an Arab confederation of nations, and South America.

It may seem incredible that the United States, the bulwark of democratic governments, could be enveloped within the Antichrist's empire, particularly if he arises from within Europe rather than from within the United States. But this will be the case, at least for a short period of time, if the Antichrist does obtain world domination. Much of his conquest of the world may not necessarily be accomplished through open warfare but by political intrigue.

Consider one possible scenario: An economic or natural catastrophe strikes the world, causing the US president to declare martial law within the United States until the trouble has passed. Increased cooperation among nations could become a necessity in order to deal with the common problem. Some of our political leaders could be bribed or coerced into acquiescing to the wishes of the Antichrist, based in the EU, in the name of such "cooperation." Such bribery of US officials could be in the form of promises of high-ranking positions in a "new world order." The Antichrist could thereby acquire more and more control of the United States until such control became absolute. He could acquire domination over other countries in a similar manner.

The Bible does not indicate in what manner the Antichrist will subdue three of the ten kingdoms (discussed earlier). Such subduing may be accomplished in a manner described above or by openly encouraging insurrection within those kingdoms. However it is accomplished, such activity may not be necessary against the remaining seven kingdoms, as they may simply submit to his authority without resistance. This seems very plausible if the three that he subdues are the three most powerful kingdoms of the ten. Each of the remaining seven may find it undesirable to confront the combined power of the three most powerful kingdoms.

It seems likely to this author that these three will turn out to be the EU, the United States, and a Russian confederation. It seems likely that other nations would be unwilling to stand up to the combined military might of these three powers.

CHAPTER 4

WORLD WAR III

The Cuban Missile Crisis

The prospect that World War III, including worldwide nuclear warfare, might take place has been feared since the 1950s. Except for the two atomic bombs that were exploded over Japan at the end of World War II, the nearest that humankind has come, so far, to engaging in nuclear warfare was the Cuban Missile Crisis in October of 1962. Russia had been shipping nuclear missiles to Cuba and installing them. Most of the United States mainland was within range of these installed missiles. US president John F. Kennedy gave Soviet premier Khrushchev an ultimatum, demanding that the Russians stop shipping such missiles to Cuba and remove the missiles already installed there. Russia blinked, and Khrushchev did what Kennedy demanded. In recent decades, military historians have become amazed at how close we came to nuclear warfare during that crisis.

Currently, there are several countries with nuclear missiles. They include the United States, Russia, Britain, France, Israel, China, India, and Pakistan. North Korea is thought to have a few nuclear warheads, but it does not yet have the means to deliver them. Iran is working on creating its first nuclear warhead.

Ezekiel's Chapters 38 and 39

There are several passages in the Bible that indicate that World War III will take place, including nuclear warfare. One such passage, which is familiar to all prophecy scholars, is in the Old Testament in Ezekiel 38–39. In these two chapters (38:15 NASB) is a description of a great army coming from the "remote parts of the north" to invade the land of Israel. The purpose of this invasion is "to capture spoil and seize plunder" (38:12). This invasion takes place "in the latter years" (38:8) and "in the last days" (38:16).

But after this invasion takes place, almighty God will have great anger against the invaders and will cause a great earthquake to take place in Israel. He will cause a "torrential rain, with hailstones, fire, and brimstone" (38:22) to rain down on the invaders. As I discuss in the chapter titled "Judgment from Heaven," this will be the result of meteors, meteorites, and an asteroid or comet raining down on the earth, rather than the side effects of nuclear weapons. Chapters 38 and 39 only describe invasions that will lead up to nuclear warfare, but not the nuclear warfare itself.

Who exactly these northern invaders will be is defined in Ezekiel 38:2–6. The leader is described as "Gog, of the land of Magog, the prince of Rosh, Meshech, and Tubal" (38:2 NASB). Accompanying him in this invasion will be Persia, Ethiopia, Put, Gomer, and Beth-togarmah.

It has been thought by many scholars for many years that Gog is the leader of Russia. One such scholar is Hal Lindsey, author of the 1970s best-selling book *The Late Great Planet Earth*. In chapter 5 of this book, Mr. Lindsey presents an excellent summary of evidence that Gog is the leader of Russia, Magog is the land of Russia, and Rosh, Meshech, and Tubal are the Russian people.[1] Mr. Lindsey cites such scholars as Herodotus, a Greek philosopher who lived in the fifth century BC; Josephus, a Jewish historian who lived in the first century AD; Pliny, a Roman writer of early Christian times; Wilhelm Gesenius, a Hebrew scholar who lived in the nineteenth century; Dr. C. F. Keil, a German scholar; and Dr. John Cumming, who lived in the nineteenth century.[2]

Mr. Lindsey claims: "For centuries, long before the current events could have influenced the interpreter's ideas, men have recognized that Ezekiel's prophecy about the northern commander referred to Russia."[3]

Another indication that Gog is the leader of Russia is the location of the land that he comes from. In my NASB Bible, Ezekiel 38:15 states that the invaders will come from the "remote parts of the north" and 39:2 says they will come from the "remotest parts of the north." If you look at any world map or globe, you can see that Russia is the country that is in the "remotest parts of the north" when compared to the location of Israel.

As for the other invaders listed in Ezekiel 38:5–6, Persia is modern-day Iran. (Its name was changed in modern times.) Ethiopia is a modern-day black African nation. According to Mr. Lindsey, the descendants of Put are the people who reside in the Arab nations of North Africa, namely Libya, Algeria, Tunisia, and Morocco.[4] Togarmah was the ancestor of the Hittites; Georgians, Armenians, and other people of the Caucasus; and the Turkic people.

As I discuss in the section "Ezekiel Chapters 38 and 39" in the chapter titled "America in Bible Prophecy," Gomer gave rise to the Germanic peoples and the Celtic peoples through his sons Ashkenaz and Riphath, respectively. The Germanic and Celtic peoples currently inhabit much of Europe and, therefore, North America—and to some extent, South America as well. The first line of Ezekiel 38:6 refers to "Gomer with *all* its troops" as participants in this invasion (emphasis mine). Therefore, *all* European and American countries that have any Germanic and/or Celtic people, including the United States, will be participants in the invasion of Israel.

Chapter 39 states that the Lord God Himself will defeat the invaders. All of the invaders will fall on the mountains of Israel. Then the Israelis will designate a burial ground for all of the invaders and will bury them in order to cleanse the land.

Toward the end of chapter 39, it states that both the Israelis and all of the Gentile nations will recognize that the Israelis were punished for their iniquities by being dispersed throughout the world, but that they have now come back to their homeland, and God will not turn His back on them anymore. This is all summarized in Ezekiel 39:27 (NASB): "When I bring them back from the peoples and gather them from the lands of their enemies, then I shall be sanctified through them in the sight of the many nations."

The Book of Joel

The Book of Joel in the Old Testament is only about four pages long, but it is filled with prophecy about end-time events. In the NASB, the phrase "the day of the Lord" is stated five times in the three chapters of Joel. (The day of the Lord is not a reference to a single day but to the general time of the second coming, and it includes events immediately prior to the second coming.)

The World War III northerners (described in Ezekiel 38 and 39) who invade Israel are described further in Joel 1:14–20 and 2:1–20. This passage states that this army marches with each soldier staying in his designated path. Verse 2:3 (NASB) indicates that either individual soldiers or the military vehicles in which some are riding will apparently use flamethrowers, as "the land is like the garden Eden before them, but a desolate wilderness behind them." Verse 2:15 (NASB) encourages the Israeli people to "consecrate a fast, proclaim a solemn assembly" because of the invasion from the north. But while Ezekiel 38–39 states that there will be a great loss of life within this army from the north, Joel 2:20 (NASB) just states that this northern army will be removed far from Israel and driven into a "parched and desolate land."

It should be noted that twice in chapter three of Joel (3:2 and 3:12) it is stated that the world's armies will be brought to the valley of Jehoshaphat, which is between the Temple Mount and the Mount of Olives on the east side of the old city of Jerusalem. This is in preparation for their battle with Christ Himself and is called the battle of Armageddon. It takes place at the time of the second coming and is not part of WWIII, which this author estimates will take place about twenty-one months before the second coming.

Revelation's Sixth Trumpet

The sixth trumpet in Revelation 9:13–21 also pertains to WWIII. It states in this passage that four angels who are bound at the Euphrates River are released so that they can kill one third of mankind through warfare. The number of "horsemen" involved in this warfare is two hundred million. Fire, smoke, and brimstone come out of the mouths of their horses. Verse 18 states that it is this fire, smoke, and brimstone that kills one third of mankind. Also, the horses' tails are like serpents, and they also do harm.

Undoubtedly, worldwide nuclear warfare takes place here, since it would be impossible to kill one third of the world's population by conventional warfare alone. As of the writing of this book, the world's population is slightly over seven billion people. One third of seven billion is two and one third billion. The number of people killed in WW II was about sixty million. So, assuming the world's population increases a bit in the next ten or fifteen years, the number of people who will be killed in WWIII will be a little over 2.33 billion, which is a little over thirty-nine times as many as the number killed in WW II.

Compare Revelation 16:12–16 with Revelation 9:13–21. While Revelation 9:13–21 refers to WWIII, Revelation 16:12–16 refers to the battle of Armageddon, which will take place at a time different from WWIII. However, many prophecy teachers think that Revelation 9:13–21 and Revelation 16:12–16 refer to the same battle or war. These teachers also think that, since the Euphrates River is mentioned in both passages, it is the kings from the east who will field large armies of two hundred million horsemen who will kill one third of the world's population.

But it is not the kings of the east who will kill one third of the world's population. The two hundred million horsemen won't all be from the kings of the east. Rather, the two hundred million are the total number of soldiers in all the world's armies. It is all the world's armies who will kill one third of the world's population, not solely the armies from the east.

Daniel's 11:40–45

Further description of World War III is found in Daniel 11:40–45. In the verses leading up to verse 40, there is a description of the activities of the Antichrist. Then, apparently at the end of the three-and-a-half-year, all-powerful activity of the

Antichrist, there will be an attack by the Arabs (the king of the south) against the Antichrist. It is not clear where the attack occurs, but they are likely to attack his headquarters in Jerusalem.

Immediately after this attack, the Russian confederation (the king of the north) also will attack the Antichrist, probably in Jerusalem. This is apparently the same Russian attack as that described in Ezekiel 38 and 39. However, Daniel 11:40–43 indicates that this is more than just an invasion of Israel. These verses indicate that Russia will invade many countries. Verse 43 states that Libya and Ethiopia will be on Russia's side.

But in verse 44, we learn that rumors from the east (probably the far east) and from the north (probably the European Union, which is the homeland of the Antichrist) disturb the Russian leader. And "he will go forth with great wrath to destroy and annihilate many." Verse 45 states that the Russian leader will establish his temporary military headquarters in Israel, but he will come to his end there. So the fate that befalls the Russian leader in Ezekiel 38 and 39 also befalls him in verse 45. That is, these two passages are in agreement as to what happens to the Russian invaders, and are referring to the same event.

Jeremiah Chapters 50 and 51

In these two chapters of Jeremiah is a long description of how the ancient city of Babylon will be brought to ruin because of the sins the Babylonians committed against the Israelis and Judeans in Old Testament times. In fact, Babylon is to become completely destroyed and completely devoid of inhabitants forever after the destruction takes place. Verse 50:32 suggests that this destruction will affect not just the city of Babylon but all of Babylonia. The Babylonia of ancient times is now the southern half of the modern nation of Iraq.

In some places in this two-chapter description, the destruction seems to refer to that inflicted upon Babylonia in Old Testament times. This includes the time the Media-Persian empire conquered the Babylonian empire. But in other places, it seems to refer to a destruction that will be inflicted in modern times. Part of this modern destruction appears to refer to World War III, and part of it appears to refer to the meteorite and asteroid/comet impacts on planet Earth, which will soon follow WWIII. (For a description of these impacts, read the chapter titled "Judgment from Heaven.")

There are apparent references to WWIII in places where it says that a military force invades Babylon from the north. These references to an army from the north are found in verses 50:3, 9, 41 and 51:48. If these verses do not refer to WWIII, then they refer to some other future conflict that will take place between the writing of this book and WWIII. As is the case with the prophecies (analyzed above) in Ezekiel, Joel, and Daniel, it seems likely that the northern commander in this prophecy in Jeremiah is the leader of Russia. I have more to say about Jeremiah 50 and 51 in the section "Jeremiah 50:41" in the chapter titled "America in Bible Prophecy."

2 Esdras Chapters 11 and 12

There appear to be other references to World War III in 2 Esdras 11:35; 12:1; and 12:28 in the Apocrypha.

In chapters 11 and 12 of 2 Esdras is a description of a large eagle with three heads, twelve large wings, and eight small wings. Verses 12:10–11 state that the eagle represents the fourth kingdom of the four kingdoms described by the prophet Daniel in the seventh chapter of the book of Daniel. The three heads represent three powerful empires that will rule the world toward the end of the life of the eagle. The small wings represent individual kings, and the large wings represent kingdoms within this fourth kingdom.

In the chapter titled "The Ten Kingdoms of the Antichrist," I stated that I think that the fourth kingdom is European civilization. I interpret the head in the center of the eagle to be the Antichrist, the head on the right to be the United States, and the head on the left to be Russia. Verse 12:27 states that the head in the center will die in bed. Verse 12:28 states that the head on the left will be killed by the head on the right, which will itself be killed in warfare. If my interpretation is correct, this means that the United States will defeat Russia in World War III. The United States will also sustain much damage through warfare, although not as much damage as that sustained by Russia. In other words, the United States will inflict more damage on Russia than the damage that Russia will inflict on the United States. Undoubtedly, nuclear warfare will play a part in this. Perhaps the United States will hit Russia without warning with a preemptive first nuclear strike. The result may be that Russia won't be able to hit the United States with much of a retaliatory response.

Read the second paragraph in the section titled "The Three Heads and the Fifth and Sixth Small Wings" in the chapter titled "The Eagle Has Landed" for further analysis of this reference.

Zechariah 14:12 and 15

In chapters 12, 13, and 14 of the book of Zechariah in the Old Testament, there is a description of warfare that is to take place in and around Jerusalem at the time of the second coming. Also contained in these three chapters are short passages that describe what will happen shortly after the second coming.

In addition, Zechariah 14:12 describes what will happen to

people who are near sites of nuclear explosions: "Now this will be the plague with which the Lord will strike all the peoples who have gone to war against Jerusalem; their flesh will rot while they stand on their feet, and their eyes will rot in their sockets, and their tongue will rot in their mouth." Evidently, this "rotting" will take place instantaneously, before their bodies have a chance to fall to the ground, due to the intense bursts of radiation at the times of the explosions. Verse 14:15 states that these terrible effects will also happen to animals that are near the sites of nuclear explosions.

Verses 14:12 and 15 seem out of place, since they pertain to the nuclear warfare that will take place in WWIII rather than in the one-sided warfare in the battle of Armageddon that takes place at the time of the second coming where Jesus defeats all the surrounding armies. (As I analyzed earlier, I estimate that WWIII will take place about twenty-one months before the second coming.) I don't have an explanation as to why the contents of verses 12 and 15 are in chapter 14, unless the intention of this three-chapter prophecy is to refer to *both* WWIII and the battle of Armageddon, since both of them will occur in "the Day of the Lord".

The Timing of World War III

As far as the timing of World War III is concerned, Ezekiel 38 indicates that it will start before the meteorite and asteroid/comet impacts take place. But Ezekiel 38 does not indicate when WWIII will come to an end in relation to these impacts.

It should be noted that WWIII may happen very fast. Conventional fighting may be engaged within a few hours or days after troop movements start, something made possible by today's mechanized means of transporting troops. The entire nuclear warfare part of WWIII may take only a few hours or days. Probably, most of the fighting will be over within a few days or weeks. The duration of the impacts will probably be only a day or two. As I calculated at the end of the chapter titled "Judgment from Heaven," these impacts will probably happen fifteen months before the second coming. It is my guess that WWIII will commence a few months before the impacts take place. If WWIII takes place about six months before these impacts do, then WWIII will take place 15 + 6 = 21 months before the second coming.

Second Esdras 11:35 and 12:1–3 give us additional knowledge about the timing of World War III. (Read the section titled "The Last Two Small Wings" in the chapter titled "The Eagle Has Landed.") Verses 11:35 and 12:1 inform us about the destruction of Russia and the partial destruction of the United States through nuclear warfare. The last two little wings, who will probably be Americans, will become leaders of the devastated fourth empire, but their reign will be very short. Then the eagle's body will burst into flames, which is representative of the widespread fires on earth caused by the meteorite and asteroid/comet strikes. In other words, first we have WWIII, then the reign of the last two small wings, and then the destruction by fire. This indicates that WWIII will both start and end before these impacts begin. If WWIII starts about six months before these impacts occur (twenty-one months before the second coming), then perhaps the last two leaders' reign will start about three months before these impacts occur (eighteen months before the second coming).

Chapter 5

Judgment from Heaven

Worldwide Destruction by Fire

Several prophetic passages in the Bible describe worldwide destruction by fire, to which the earth and its inhabitants will be subjected at the end of this age, shortly before the second coming of Jesus Christ. For example, consider 2 Peter 3:10 (NASB): "But the day of the Lord will come like a thief, in which the heavens will pass away with a roar and the elements will be destroyed with intense heat, and the earth and its works will be burned up."

Other examples include 2 Peter 3:12; Revelation 8:7; 16:8–9; Ezekiel 38:22; 39:6; Joel 1:19–20; 2:30; Zephaniah 1:18; Malachi 4:1; Isaiah 29:6; 30:30; 66:15–16; and 2 Esdras 12:3 in the Apocrypha.

When I first read these passages some thirty-five years before the writing of this book, what first occurred to me was that these passages were referring to World War III, including worldwide nuclear warfare. But since then, it has occurred to me that these passages are actually referring to billions of rocks from outer space, specifically meteors, meteorites, and a mountain-sized asteroid or comet bombarding the earth.

One reason for thinking that these passages do not refer to WWIII is that they seem to refer to a worldwide tribulation of sorts that involves all lands throughout the world. The use of nuclear weapons in WWIII, on the other hand, will involve only some countries, not all countries. For example, the developing countries in South America and sub-Saharan Africa will not be hit by nuclear weapons, since they have no enemies with nuclear weapons. Also, in the countries that are hit by nuclear weapons, only cities and military sites will be targeted. The rural areas will, for the most part, escape this destruction—although it is possible that some of the nuclear missiles will go off course, and strike rural areas rather than the cities they were programmed to hit.

Meteors are tiny rocks, the size of a pea or smaller, that ablate completely from air friction when they enter the earth's atmosphere. Ablation is a process where the outer surface of a meteor or meteorite gets very hot, melts, and boils off because of air friction. (It is not the same thing as "burning," where a substance is broken down chemically and combined with oxygen atoms.)

Meteorites are rocks from outer space that are larger than meteors. They can be up to several tons in weight, although the vast majority of meteorites weigh only a few pounds. Only the outer surface of a meteorite ablates in the atmosphere. The part of the meteorite that does not ablate hits the ground.

An *asteroid* is any rock in the solar system that is larger than ten meters in diameter. The majority of asteroids are between ten and one hundred meters in diameter. The largest asteroid in the solar system is a little over six hundred miles in diameter.

Comets have been referred to as "dirty snowballs." They are mostly made up of frozen water and other frozen compounds, and they have rocks of various sizes embedded in them. Comets are typically one or more miles in diameter.

The Bible verse that suggests that the earth will be hit by either a comet or an asteroid is Revelation 8:8 (NASB): "And the second angel sounded, and something like a great mountain burning with fire was thrown into the sea; and a third of the sea became blood."

The meteors and meteorites described above are usually in the orbits of extinct comets, which the earth periodically passes through, and the "mountain burning with fire" quoted above may be an asteroid that was embedded in a comet before it became extinct. Or it may be that the burning mountain is what is left of a comet that is not yet extinct. (An extinct comet is what is left after all the frozen water and other frozen compounds have evaporated after many orbits around the sun. That is, what is left is a large number of rocks of all sizes, which used to be embedded in the comet and which still go around the sun in the original orbit of the comet.) Whatever this burning mountain is, either an asteroid or comet, it is apparently several thousand feet in diameter.

Definition of the Word *Hail*

One reason for thinking that rocks from outer space will be the cause of worldwide destruction by fire is the usage of the word *hail* in the Bible. It appears that passages containing the word *hail* refer to a hail of rocks rather than the small pellets of ice we normally think of.

For example, consider Revelation 8:7 (NASB), which refers to the first trumpet: "And the first sounded, and there came hail and fire, mixed with blood, and they were thrown to the earth; and a third of the earth was burnt up, and a third of the trees were burnt up, and all the green grass was burnt up."

The word *hail* in this verse probably refers to the meteors, which ablate completely as they travel down through the atmosphere at a high velocity, and to meteorites, which are only partially ablated before they reach the ground. The word *fire* refers to the fact that these meteors and meteorites are ablating. We don't see fire when we see a hail of ice pellets fall to the ground. But we would see meteors and meteorites ablating in the atmosphere if the word *hail* is referring to numerous meteors and meteorites. The word *fire* may also refer to nitrogen burning in the atmosphere, which is heated up by the meteors and meteorites. The word *blood* probably refers to the chemical compound nitrogen dioxide (NO_2), which has a reddish brown color (the approximate color of blood) and is created when nitrogen burns in the atmosphere. (See the discussion about NO_2 in the next section of this chapter.)

Another reason for thinking that "hail" is referring to rocks or stones is apparent after reading chapters 7 through 12 in Exodus. These chapters describe the plagues that the Egyptians had to suffer when Moses was trying to get Pharaoh to let the Hebrew people leave Egypt. These plagues took place in approximately 1450 BC.

By coincidence, this is the same approximate time when the second or third most powerful volcanic explosion in recorded history took place. This explosion occurred on the island of Thera in the Aegean Sea between Greece and Asia Minor. The explosion almost completely destroyed Thera. It left only a few remnants of it, which are now called the Santorini Islands. It appears that some of the plagues that the Egyptians had to endure can be attributed to this volcanic explosion.

For example, some geologists think that the large amount of volcanic ash created by the explosion may have caused the plague of darkness in Egypt. This is not surprising, since it is known that some other volcanic eruptions have spewed out large amounts of ash, which has caused temporary periods of darkness. Verse 10:21 states that the darkness is "even a darkness which may be felt." And volcanic ash is something which can be felt as it gradually falls to the ground.

One of the Egyptian plagues was "hail." (See Exodus 9:18–26.) Ice pellets are not produced by volcanic explosions. But a hail of volcanic rocks, such as pumice stones, cinder, and blocks, is produced by volcanic explosions. The hail is described as being life-threatening. That is, the Egyptians were warned to get all of their servants and livestock into shelter lest they be killed by the hail. This is more characteristic of volcanic rocks than of ice pellets. So in these verses, *hail* must be referring to volcanic rocks rather than ice pellets, and the volcanic explosion on Thera is implicated.

The idea that *hail* is referring to volcanic rocks in this passage of Exodus is further supported by the following analysis. Exodus 9:23 (NASB) states that when the Lord sent thunder and hail over Egypt, "fire ran down to the earth." This fire must be referencing the fact that the hailstones haven't yet cooled off as they fall to the ground at high speed. This is characteristic of volcanic rocks rather than ice pellets. The word *fire* may also refer to nitrogen burning in the atmosphere, which is heated up by the volcanic rocks as they fall down through the atmosphere. Also, verse 9:24 refers to fire "flashing continually in the midst of the hail." Here also, volcanic rocks are indicated. Apparently, the centers of the rocks haven't cooled off yet, so in the centers of these rocks ("in the midst") there is still some molten lava. And verse 9:25 states that the hail "shattered every tree of the field," once again implicating volcanic rocks rather than small ice pellets.

The idea that some of these plagues were caused by

a volcanic explosion is further supported by the following discussion. Three other plagues may have been caused by the volcanic explosion on Thera.

1. The plague of water turned into blood, mentioned in Exodus 7, might have been nitrogen dioxide (NO_2) produced when volcanic rocks fell down through the atmosphere at high speed—in a manner similar to when the meteors and meteorites will come down through the atmosphere during the tribulation (Rev. 8:7). All the bodies of water, including the Nile River, where the rocks fell would have a reddish-brown tint produced by the NO_2, thus giving them the appearance of blood. (See the description of NO_2 in the next section.)

2. All of the pollutants in Egypt, including the volcanic rocks and volcanic ash, could have caused the plague of frogs and the plague of insects. The rocks and ash could have caused the frogs and insects to leave the territory where they naturally resided and invade the residences where the Egyptian people lived and worked. That insects and other animals could be so adversely affected by volcanoes is demonstrated by a volcano that exploded on Mount Pelee on the island of Martinique in the Caribbean Sea on May 8, 1902.

In the days leading up to this eruption, at a sugar mill just outside of the Martinique city of St. Pierre, there was an invasion of thousands of ants and centipedes that had been driven down the slopes of the volcano by the volcanic ash (which was already coming out of the volcano in small amounts) and the rumblings of the volcano. Also, in a district in St. Pierre, there was an invasion of poisonous snakes. If the snakes and insects were so adversely affected by the volcanic ash on Mount Pelee, then maybe the frogs and insects in Egypt were similarly affected by the ash from the volcano on Thera, thus causing the plague of frogs and the plague of insects.

3. The plague of boils might have been brought about when the volcanic ash gradually fell out of the sky onto the Egyptian people and their animals.

Therefore, it seems likely that the three plagues discussed above were caused by the volcanic explosion on Thera, and that the references to "hail" in Exodus 9 are references to volcanic rocks rather than pellets of ice. This in turn makes it plausible that other biblical references to "hail" mean falling rocks.

Side Effects from Bombardment by Meteors, Meteorites, and the Asteroid or Comet

The side effects of this bombardment will be catastrophic. As a result of the meteors and meteorites shooting through the atmosphere, the earth's atmosphere will temporarily become very hot. The hot air will kill land vegetation throughout the world and cause it to dry out. The pollutants from the ablating rocks in the atmosphere will cause lightning strikes from the air to the ground, thereby setting the dried vegetation on fire. Consequently, there will be vast forest fires and grass fires throughout the world. Also, many buildings will catch fire.

The word *blood* in Revelation 8:7–8 probably refers to the chemical compound nitrogen dioxide (NO_2), which is created when the meteors, meteorites, and asteroid or comet travel down through the atmosphere at very high speeds. The atmosphere is 78 percent free nitrogen and 21 percent free oxygen. The free nitrogen and free oxygen in the atmosphere are heated up by these rocks so that some of the nitrogen burns and becomes chemically bonded with oxygen to produce NO_2. Nitrogen dioxide has a reddish-brown color, which is almost the color of blood.

When the asteroid or comet strikes the sea or ocean, much NO_2 will be produced in the plume, or fireball, above the point of impact. The NO_2 will eventually be washed out of the atmosphere by rain and will acidify all bodies of water it falls in. (See Revelation 16:4.) Also, if the asteroid or comet hits an ocean floor that contains sulfates, then sulfur dioxide (SO_2) and sulfur trioxide (SO_3) released from the sulfates will contribute to the acidification of oceans and other bodies of water. The extremely large tsunamis and the churning of the sea produced by the impact and ocean currents will spread the NO_2, SO_2, and SO_3 throughout the sea or ocean (or at least one third of it). Over a period of several weeks, ocean currents and the continued churning of the oceans will gradually spread this tainted, acidic water throughout all of the world's oceans and saltwater seas, giving them the appearance of blood. (See Revelation 16:3.)

In Revelation 8:9, it says that one third of all sea creatures will die. This may refer to all sea creatures in the particular ocean or sea that the asteroid or comet hits, or one third of all sea creatures in all of the world's oceans and seas. This sea life may be killed by an extremely powerful shock wave that travels throughout that ocean or sea, or by the water pollutants that are produced by the impact.

Verse 9 also states that one third of all the ships will flounder. This could include all the ships in that particular ocean or sea, or one third of all the ships in all the world's oceans and seas. They may flounder because of massive tsunamis hundreds or thousands of feet high, which go out in all directions from the point of impact. Also, the tsunamis will go ashore on all lands that have a shoreline on that particular ocean or sea, wreaking havoc on all towns, villages, and cities within a few hundred miles of the coast.

Ocean water will churn vigorously, and smaller tsunamis will travel as eddies throughout the other oceans. (See Luke 21:25.) The NO_2, acid, and other water pollutants caused by the impact will gradually spread throughout all of the world's oceans and saltwater seas and cause the deaths of all sea creatures in those bodies of water. (See Revelation 16:3.)

When the comet or asteroid strikes a sea or ocean, it will blast out a temporary crater in the water, several thousand feet wide and several thousand feet deep. The question is: will a crater be created in the ocean floor? That is to say, will the object have enough momentum to strike the ocean floor very hard underneath the ocean? If the object is small and the water where it hits is deep, then the sea or ocean floor will not be hit hard. But if the object is large and the water is shallow, then the object will strike the ocean floor very hard and create a crater in the ocean floor.

In either case, a huge amount of water will be blasted high above the atmosphere and will fall back down to earth hundreds and thousands of miles away. If some of the sea or ocean floor is also blasted up above the atmosphere when a crater is created in the ocean floor, then rocks of all sizes could come raining down all over the earth. Large quantities of dust would be blasted into the atmosphere. A giant fireball hundreds of miles in diameter would be created and expand in all directions away from the point of impact.

The asteroid or comet itself will be blasted into small pieces, which will go above the atmosphere and come raining down hundreds and thousands of miles away. Possibly these rocks raining back down to earth are referred to in Revelation 8:10

where it says that a great star fell from heaven. As the rocks shoot up through the atmosphere and then fall back to earth, their surfaces will ablate in the atmosphere. The mixture of NO_2, SO_2, SO_3, and water in the atmosphere will cause the water to become very acidic and fall back to earth as acid rain. This rain will be so acidic that people will die from using or drinking water from any river or spring that has been polluted by the rainwater. It may be that this rainwater is the torrential rain mentioned in Ezekiel 38:22. Possibly, metals and other chemical elements will be leached from the fallen hot rocks into the fresh water, adding to its toxicity (Revelation 8:10–11).

There will be many pollutants in the atmosphere due to the ablation of meteors, meteorites, and rocks blasted away from the asteroid or comet impact; the smoke and soot produced from burning forests, grasses, and buildings; and the WWIII nuclear warfare that will have taken place a few months before the meteorite and asteroid/comet impacts. The result will be that sunlight and moonlight will be reduced by one third, and the surface of the earth will become cold. (See Revelation 8:12; Matthew 24:29; and Joel 2:31.)

There appear to be more references to the asteroid or comet impact in the seventh bowl of wrath near the end of chapter 16 in Revelation. Verse 18 makes a reference to the most powerful earthquake there has ever been since mankind has been on the face of the earth. (The impact of the asteroid or comet will produce an extremely powerful earthquake, which will be felt throughout the entire world.) Verse 19 indicates that many of the buildings in cities throughout the world will collapse because of that earthquake.

Verse 20 also appears to refer to a consequence of that earthquake. The earthquake will be so powerful that all of the earth's mountains will sink into the earth's crust, causing them to "not be found." Islands that are the tops of mountains on the ocean floor will apparently sink beneath sea level. Verse 21 has a reference to hailstones, about one hundred pounds each, falling on the earth. The fact that these hailstones weigh about a hundred pounds each suggests that they are rocks rather than pellets of ice. (Also see Ezekiel 38:19–20.)

That an asteroid or comet impact could produce such a powerful earthquake becomes clear after reading the book titled *Rogue Asteroids and Doomsday Comets* by Duncan Steel, PhD, an Australian astronomer. On page 1 of this book, Dr. Steel describes what would happen if a large asteroid were to strike southern California. In addition to lumps raining down on Hawaii and New York, Dr. Steel notes: "Not that Honolulu or New York City would be left standing by then. Phenomenal seismic shocks following the impact would have already shaken them flat."[1]

On the first page of chapter three there is a similar statement. Dr. Steel remarks about what would happen if an asteroid five hundred meters in diameter struck the outback in Australia. "For example, if the asteroid fell in the Outback, all of the cities in Australia would almost surely be shaken flat."[2]

Still more references to meteors, meteorites, and an asteroid or comet are in Revelation 6:12–14. Verse 12 mentions a great earthquake, the sun not shining because of pollutants in the atmosphere, and the moon appearing like blood because of the NO_2 in the atmosphere. Verse 13 mentions stars (meteors and meteorites) falling from the sky like figs shaken out of a fig tree. Verse 14 mentions that the sky was split apart, and "every mountain and island were moved out of their places." The sky being split apart may be a phenomenon that will occur when the asteroid or comet blasts through the atmosphere on its way to the surface of the earth. Every mountain and island being "moved out of their places" will happen as a result of the powerful earthquake that will be generated when the comet or asteroid strikes an ocean or sea and (possibly) the ocean floor.

I suspect, but I am not certain, that Revelation 8:8 is referring to an asteroid rather than a comet. This is because the earth is hit by asteroids much more often than by comets. Because of this uncertainty, when I refer to the phenomena described in Revelation 8:7–8 in other chapters of this book, I will use the phrase "meteorite and asteroid/comet impacts."

Past Impacts by Asteroids and Comets

It wasn't until a few decades ago that scientists realized that the earth might be hit by asteroids and comets. There aren't many craters on planet Earth that are easily recognized as being caused by asteroid or comet impacts. But now that scientists realize that the earth has been hit in the past and will occasionally be hit in the future, they are looking for telltale craters caused by such impacts. It was in the 1950s when scientists started to realize that the numerous craters on the moon were caused by asteroid and comet impacts rather than volcanoes.

So far, scientists have found more than two hundred impact craters on the earth's surface. These craters on the earth's surface are not easy to spot. This is due to water and wind erosion and also to the growth of vegetation over all land masses (except Antarctica), which tends to disguise craters. Some craters that were once thought to be extinct volcanoes are now thought to be impact craters. Craters on the ocean floors are difficult or impossible to detect, and three fourths of the earth's surface is covered by water.

Still another reason why not many craters have been found is that some of the earth's crust is being, and has been, destroyed by being gradually shoved down into the earth's mantle. This process, known as plate tectonics, also destroys craters that were in affected parts of the earth's crust. A reader's study of plate tectonics can aid in the understanding of this.

One well-known crater, the Barringer Meteorite Crater (also known as Meteor Crater), is about 1.2 kilometers across. This crater was caused by a small nickel-iron asteroid, about 150 feet in diameter, that smashed into a region in northern Arizona about fifty thousand years ago.

Another crater—or, I should say, *remnants* of a crater—was discovered in the 1980s, centered on the shoreline of the Yucatan Peninsula in Mexico. Half of the crater is in the Yucatan Peninsula, and the other half is underneath the Gulf of Mexico. The persons who found this crater were looking for good locations to drill for oil, and they happened to find this crater. It wasn't easy to detect, since the crater had been created sixty-five million years ago and had been covered by sediment deposited there throughout that long period of time. Scientists were able to calculate that this crater, which is 120 miles in diameter, was created by the impact of an asteroid six miles in diameter.

By coincidence, sixty-five million years ago was when the Cretaceous geological era came to a close and the Tertiary era started. At this boundary, many species of plants and animals became extinct, including the dinosaurs, and many new species came into existence. It is now thought by many scientists that the end of the Cretaceous era and the beginning of the Tertiary era were caused by this asteroid impact.

A much more recent encounter between an asteroid and planet Earth occurred on June 30, 1908. An asteroid exploded in the atmosphere over the Tungus River region of Siberia in Russia. Since the asteroid did not hit the ground, no crater was created. It exploded in the atmosphere because it was traveling downward at a very high velocity of several miles per second. The air in front of the asteroid did not have time to move out from in front of the asteroid, so the air became very compressed very quickly. Eventually, it was like hitting a brick wall, and the asteroid exploded in midair.

The asteroid is estimated to have been fifty to sixty meters in diameter. About 1,200 square miles of forest were destroyed by a blast wave and a powerful flash of heat radiation that proceeded from the site of the explosion. The blast wave bent over many trees, and the flash of extreme heat set many of them on fire instantaneously. Many reindeer were incinerated. Since this was a remote region, very few people were injured. There were no human deaths.

Even more recent was the explosion of another asteroid in the atmosphere over Russia (yes, Russia was hit again) in February of 2013. The asteroid was estimated to have been about fifty feet in diameter. The explosion caused a shock wave that shattered many windows in the buildings below. Numerous people sustained injuries from the flying glass.

Currently, big rocks the size of a car or a small house periodically enter our atmosphere and explode in the upper atmosphere. Such explosions are detected by our military satellites. The characteristics of these explosions are such that the US Department of Defense realizes that they are from large boulders, not nuclear weapons.

Attempt to Protect the Earth from Future Impacts

Now that planetary scientists have accepted the fact that the earth occasionally gets hit by asteroids and comets, some of them are now actively searching for near-earth objects, or NEOs. NEOs are asteroids and comets that come close to the earth in their orbits around the sun. When such an object is detected, its orbit for several years in the future is calculated to see if it is on a collision course with the earth. So far, many NEOs have been found, but none are on a collision course with the earth. If such an NEO is found, then the human race will have to take some action to prevent that NEO from striking the planet.

One possible way to prevent the object from hitting the earth is to hit it with a nuclear warhead. One strategy calls for blasting the object into smaller pieces. Another strategy calls for merely nudging the object so that its orbit is changed slightly and it misses the earth. These two plans are currently being considered by scientists. Much research and technical development needs to be done before mankind will be able to strike an NEO and produce the desired effect.

Failure to Protect the Earth

If Revelation 8:8 really is a biblical prophecy that describes the earth being struck by an asteroid or comet, then somehow, in order for the prophecy to come true, our efforts at neutralizing this object must fail. One of the following will happen:

- a system to intercept such objects will not yet have been developed
- the object will not be detected in time to intercept it
- the system will in some way fail to successfully intercept the object

The Timing of the Meteorite and Asteroid/Comet Impacts

The time when these impacts take place in relation to the second coming is revealed in Daniel 7:11–12 (NASB). These two verses state that the fourth beast (empire) of Daniel 7 will be destroyed and given to a fire, and an extension of life will be given to the first three beasts (empires) "for an appointed period of time." The *New International Version* of the Bible states "for a period of time" rather than "for an appointed period of time." The *King James Version* states "for a season and time," and the *Amplified Bible* states "for a season and a time." The KJV and AB have the most exact translations of the phrase in question, and therefore, they are probably the most accurate translations.

But what is "a season and a time"? In a few places in the book of Daniel, the word *time* is used in place of the word *year*. That appears to be the case here also. One year is twelve months long. A season is three months long. Therefore, a season and a time are three months plus twelve months, or fifteen months. Apparently, this destruction of the fourth empire is going to take place as a result of the meteorite and asteroid/comet impacts, and the other three empires are going to exist right up until the second coming. Therefore, these impacts will take place fifteen months before the second coming.

Chapter 6

The Timing of the Rapture

In the Bible, there are apparent references to a rapture, an event where Jesus will return to the earth's atmosphere and cause the church to leave the earth and join Him in the air. For example, see 1 Thessalonians 4:13–18. The Bible does not clearly state when the rapture will take place relative to other events in the latter years.

There are currently four schools of thought as to when the rapture will take place. Adherents of all four believe in the premillennialist view. That is, they believe that the rapture and the second coming of Christ will take place before the millennium, the last thousand-year period before the last judgment by almighty God. Also, all four schools of thought believe that the second coming will take place after the tribulation.

When the rapture will occur relative to the tribulation is the point where they differ. The pretribulationist view is that the rapture will occur before the tribulation. The midtribulationist view is that the rapture will occur in the middle of the tribulation. The posttribulationist view is that the rapture will occur after the tribulation—at the same time as the second coming. The pre-wrath view states that God's wrath upon the earth will begin sometime during the second half of Daniel's seventieth week of years, and that the rapture will take place just before it.

It should be pointed out that no matter which view is the correct view, some saved people may be killed during the tribulation. Most prophecy commentators nowadays believe in the pretribulationist view.

The Tribulation

I need to say a few things about the tribulation before I continue discussing the rapture.

I looked in my concordance of the King James Version of the Bible and found out that in the KJV Bible there are twenty-two references to a tribulation where the word *tribulation* is actually used.[1] However, only four of these twenty-two references refer to an apparent worldwide tribulation that takes place just before the second coming. They are in Matthew 24:21, 29; Mark 13:24; and Revelation 7:14. (The other eighteen references refer to other times of trials and tribulations that individuals or nations go through in life.) As for these four references to a worldwide latter-year tribulation, the Bible does not state what it will consist of or how long it will last.

In two of these four verses, Matthew 24:21 and Revelation 7:14, the term *great tribulation* is used, while in the other two verses, the term *tribulation* is used. After reading these four passages, it is not apparent to me that the "great tribulation" is in any way different from the "tribulation." For example, it is not apparent that the "great tribulation" is the second half of the "tribulation," which is the way some prophecy scholars like to define "great tribulation."

Also, there are many other apparent references to the tribulation where the word *tribulation* is not used. There are many references in both the Old and New Testaments to vast fires in the latter years. For an example, see 2 Peter 3:7–12. Also, there are descriptions in Revelation of terrible things that will happen to the world in the latter years, which surely will be part of the tribulation.

There are three phenomena: one, two, or all three of which might be included in the tribulation, depending upon God's definition of the tribulation. The last one to occur, the meteorite and asteroid/comet impacts, is surely part of the tribulation because of the severity of its effects on the earth and the great loss of life it will cause. Read the chapter titled "Judgment from Heaven" for a description of this.

The phenomenon of World War III will occur a few months before these impacts and will kill one third of mankind. And before WWIII, the Antichrist will reign for three and a half years, during which time he will be allowed to do anything he wishes to do, including taking over the entire world. (See Revelation 13:5, 7.) Note that the Antichrist's control over Europe will begin sometime before this three-and-a-half-year period begins.

As I discussed in the last section of the chapter titled "Judgment from Heaven," I believe that the meteorite and asteroid/comet impacts will occur about fifteen months before the second coming. I also estimate that the start of WWIII will be about six months before these impacts, or twenty-one months before the second coming. If the three-and-a-half-year reign of the Antichrist ends exactly when WWIII starts, then it will begin about three and a half years plus twenty-one months, or five years and three months before the second coming.

The duration of the meteorite and asteroid/comet impacts surely won't be very long, perhaps a few hours or a few days. The question that arises is this: is the time period between the last of these impacts and the second coming (which will be fifteen months long) to be considered part of the tribulation? Matthew 24:29 seems to suggest that there will be an abrupt end to the tribulation, after which the sun and the moon will be darkened, the stars will "fall" from the sky, and the heavens will be shaken. So, maybe the tribulation ends when the last impact takes place. On the other hand, I can't see how the time period between the last impact and the second coming wouldn't be part of the tribulation, since it would surely be a hell on earth to live through. I don't know the answer to this question, so I'll leave it unanswered.

Of course, we humans can arbitrarily choose our own definitions of the tribulation—or the great tribulation. But if we do so, we should keep it in mind that our opinions may differ from the definition that God uses in the four verses cited above.

When the rapture will take place relative to the second coming in the pretribulationist, midtribulationist, and pre-wrath viewpoints is dependent upon the definition of *tribulation*. For example, suppose that the pretribulationist viewpoint is the correct viewpoint. If the tribulation consists only of the meteorite and asteroid/comet impacts (although the reign of the Antichrist and WWIII will still happen), then the rapture will take place on or before a date fifteen months before the second coming. If the tribulation consists of these impacts and also WWIII, then the rapture will take place on or before a date twenty-one months before the second coming. If the tribulation also includes the three-and-a-half-year reign of the Antichrist, then the rapture will take place on or before a date five years and three months before the second coming.

Most prophecy commentators believe that the tribulation will last for seven years. However, there is no reference to a seven-year tribulation in the Bible. There are, however, two references to two seven-year periods in the latter years (and thus two reasons for believing in a seven-year tribulation) in the Bible.

One of the references to a latter-year, seven-year time period is in Ezekiel 39:9–10. This passage states that for a period of seven years the Israelis will make fires with the weapons of Gog and all his followers after the latter-year battle of Gog and many other peoples in the land of Israel (which will be a part of WWIII). A few people don't think that this burning of Gog's weapons will take place for seven years after the second coming. Rather, they believe that this great battle will take place seven years before the second coming so that this burning of the weapons will be finished by the time the second coming takes place. And they believe the tribulation must start when this battle takes place, seven years before the second coming. However, there isn't anything wrong with the Israelis burning these weapons for seven years after the second coming. It would be an act of cleansing the land, just as burying all the dead bodies of that great battle for a period of seven months is an act of cleansing the land as described in Ezekiel 39:11–16.

The other reference to a seven-year period in the latter years is in Daniel 9:27, a verse that describes the last "week" of seven years of Daniel's seventy weeks of years. (See the chapter titled "An Analysis of Daniel's Seventy Weeks of Years.") According to this verse, the Antichrist will make a covenant with many peoples for a period of seven years. In the middle of this "week," he will put a stop to sacrifice and grain offerings at the new Israeli temple in Jerusalem. This seven-year period will take place immediately before the second coming.

Some people see that the Antichrist will apparently be in power as far back as seven years before the second coming. (He may have control over Europe, but he won't have control over the whole world yet.) They think that things will be "pretty bad," as the Antichrist is already a world leader at that point. So, they think that the tribulation will start when the Antichrist makes this pact seven years before the second coming, and that the tribulation will last that entire seven years. (However, it should be noted that things won't be "too bad" during the first year and nine months of this seven-year period. There will be some warfare between Europe and the Middle East but no worldwide calamities. See the chapter titled "The Last Seven Years Before the Second Coming of Jesus Christ.")

Some prophecy teachers believe that the three-and-a-half-year reign of the Antichrist coincides with the last three and a years of the so-called seven-year tribulation. Because of this, and because they believe WWIII will take place near the end of this time period, they arbitrarily call the last three and a half years the "great tribulation." However, the three-and-a-half-year reign of the Antichrist cannot coincide with the last three and a half years before the second coming. There are two reasons for thinking this.

First of all, the abomination of desolation of the Israeli temple in Jerusalem in the latter years, which will take place at the midpoint of the seven-year period, will last only 1,150 days, not 1,260 days (three and a half years). (See Daniel 8:9–14; 11:31. Note that 2,300 evenings and mornings are equivalent to 1,150 twenty-four-hour time periods.) After the 1,150 days have passed, the temple will be restored, and the daily animal sacrifices and grain offerings will resume as the Israelis resume their worship of God.

But the Antichrist would never stand for such a resumption of temple rituals. He would prevent it if he had the power to do so. That is to say, he would prevent such a resumption if the temple priests attempted it during the Antichrist's three-and-a-half-year reign. So the Antichrist's three-and-a-half-year reign must end either on or before the 1,150-day mark, which is 110 days sooner than the 1,260-day mark. (He may retain control over Europe but lose control over the Middle East and the rest of the world.) Therefore, the start of his three-and-a-half-year reign must be at least three and a half years plus 110 days, or three years and 292 days before the second coming, rather than three and a half years before the second coming.

Secondly, Scripture seems to indicate that WWIII and the meteorite and asteroid/comet impacts will take place approximately twenty-one months and fifteen months, respectively, before the second coming. Surely the reign of the Antichrist will end on or before the date that WWIII starts (twenty-one months before the second coming), since he will no longer have control over the world after WWIII starts. So, if the pretribulationist view is the correct view, and the tribulation includes the three-and-a-half-year reign of the Antichrist, then the start of his reign, and the rapture, would be at least twenty-one months plus three and a half years, or five years and three months before the second coming.

The Rapture

After having read all of the passages about the rapture in the Bible, it is my impression that the posttribulationist view is the correct view. For one thing, the Bible does not state that the rapture and second coming will be two separate events. Another reason for thinking this is a passage in the Olivet Discourse in Matthew 24:29–31. This clearly states that, in this chronological order, first the tribulation, then the second coming, and then the rapture will take place.

Some pretribulationist commentators state that the rapture

in verse 31 is a rapture of the tribulation saints and/or the saved Jewish people and that the rapture of the church will still happen before the tribulation. But this would mean that there are going to be two raptures, and the Bible makes no mention of the fact that there will be two raptures before the millennium.

There is another passage in the Bible that implies that the rapture will take place at the same time as, or immediately after, the second coming. It is Revelation 20:4–6. In this passage, there is a description of two resurrections. Verse 4 states that there will be a resurrection of Christians who were beheaded because of the testimony of Jesus or because of the Word of God. Also included in this resurrection will be those who will be given the opportunity to worship the Antichrist but will choose not to do so. Verse 5 states that the resurrection described in verse 4 is the "first resurrection." It also states in verse 5 that the rest of the dead will not come to life until after a thousand years have passed. Presumably, at that time there will be a second resurrection.

Another passage in the Bible that appears to describe the rapture is 1 Thessalonians 4:13–18. In fact, the prevailing view in Christian eschatology is that this passage is describing the rapture. This passage states in verse 16 that "the dead in Christ will rise first," and then in verse 17 that Christians who are still alive will rise and join them "in the clouds, to meet the Lord in the air" (NASB). Thus, this passage states that all Christians who are either dead or alive will rise to meet the Lord in the air. Since verse 16 states that dead people will be included in this rapture, and Revelation 20:4 states that the so-called "first resurrection" is the first resurrection that includes dead people, these two passages must be referring to the same event.

The fact that the first resurrection will include people

who choose not to worship the Antichrist implies that this resurrection will be at least as late as the end of the three-and-a-half-year reign of the Antichrist, which I estimated in a previous chapter to be about twenty-one months before the second coming. Thus the notion that the rapture will happen seven years before the second coming appears to be incorrect.

As I stated earlier, Matthew 24:29–31 states that the rapture will take place immediately after the second coming. Furthermore, the events described in chapters 19 and 20 of Revelation appear to happen in chronological order. The second coming is discussed in chapter 19, so the resurrection discussed in 20:4–6 appears to happen immediately after the second coming.

Thus the one—and only one—rapture will take place immediately after the second coming. It follows that the posttribulationist view is the correct view when considering the timing of the rapture.

One reason why the pretribulationist view is so popular is that there is simply a desire among Christians not to have to live through the tribulation. To some Christians, it would seem unfair for Christians to have to live through this terrible time period after having already repented of their sins and accepted Jesus Christ as their Lord and Savior. But we have to go by what the Bible says, not by what we want. After all, Jesus said in the New Testament that we have to pick up our cross and follow Him. In other words, things are difficult in this life but we have to try to live through it.

Some prophecy commentators have cited 2 Thessalonians 5:9 as an indication that good Christians won't have to live through the tribulation (and thus that the pretribulationist view is the correct view). But I believe that the word *wrath* in this verse refers to being sentenced to the lake of fire at the last judgment, not the tribulation. Thus good Christians will escape being sentenced to the lake of fire, but they won't necessarily escape having to live through the tribulation.

Also, some commentators have cited Revelation 3:10 as an indication that Christians won't have to live through the "hour of testing," i.e., the tribulation. However, this message was meant for just one of the seven churches, not all of them. Also, Revelation 3:10 may mean that some Christians won't have to live through the tribulation, while other Christians will. Some Christians may lose their lives during the tribulation, while others may successfully live through it.

In Revelation 7:9–17, there is a description of a great multitude of saved people from every nation, tribe, and tongue, which no one can count, who have "come out of" the tribulation. In order for them to come out of the tribulation, they must first enter it. These people apparently were either killed during the tribulation or successfully lived through it. They were not included in any rapture that took place before the tribulation. So, this passage also indicates that there will be no pretribulation rapture. One could argue that the main rapture will still be before the tribulation, but there are apparently so many people cited in Revelation 7:9–17 (a great multitude) that this seems unlikely.

We shall have to wait until the final seven years before the second coming to see if my reasoning in this chapter is correct.

Chapter 7

The Second Coming

One time when I attended a Bible study class many years ago, one of the participants put forth the theory that the expression "the second coming of Jesus Christ" means that Jesus will come into your life once you accept Him as your Lord and Savior. It is true that Jesus will establish a relationship with you when you repent of your sins and accept Him as your Lord and Savior. But what is meant by "the second coming" is an actual, physical, bodily return of Jesus Christ to planet Earth. It will be a grand and glorious event, witnessed by everybody throughout the world, both living and dead. (See Revelation 1:7.) When Christ returns, He will rule over the entire earth from Jerusalem for one thousand years. This will be followed by a day of judgment, when almighty God will decide who goes to heaven and who is sentenced to the lake of fire.

When Christ was on the earth the first time, He fulfilled a number of Old Testament prophecies about Himself. When He comes back again, He will fulfill the Old Testament prophecies about Himself that He did not fulfill the first time He was on earth. He will also fulfill many prophecies about Himself in the New Testament.

The second coming is one of the most prominent doctrines

in the Bible, second only to the doctrine of salvation.[1] According to *The Popular Encyclopedia of Bible Prophecy* edited by Tim Lahaye and Ed Hindson, there are 321 references to the second coming in the New Testament.[2] In the Old Testament, the second coming is referred to in several of the psalms and by all of the prophets.[3] In the New Testament, all of the apostles refer to it, and so does Jesus on several occasions.[4] It is mentioned in twenty-three of the twenty-seven New Testament books.[5] The second coming is referred to in each chapter of 1 and 2 Thessalonians.[6] Specifically, it is mentioned in 1 Thessalonians 1:10; 2:19; 3:13; 4:14–16; 5:23; and in 2 Thessalonians 1:7, 10; and 2:1, 8.

In the rest of this chapter, I discuss some of the more prominent references to the second coming.

Zechariah

Zechariah, one of the minor prophets in the Old Testament, had quite a bit to say about the general time period of the second coming in chapters 12, 13, and 14 of his Old Testament book. In Zechariah 12:10–14, he describes a great mourning in the land of Israel over Jesus, as the Israelis look at Jesus (during the second coming), whom they once pierced. Verses 8 and 9 of chapter 13 describe how one third of the land of Israel will be saved. Verses 3 and 4 of chapter 14 mention that the Lord will go and fight all the nations' armies that have gathered around Jerusalem.

The Olivet Discourse

The Olivet Discourse is a passage in three of the four Gospels in the New Testament in which Jesus explained to His disciples the things that would take place in the future, including at the time of the second coming. It is called the Olivet Discourse because it was a discourse given by Jesus while He and His disciples were on the Mount of Olives. The full discourse is presented in Matthew 24 and 25. Abbreviated versions of it are in Mark 13 and Luke 21.

The second coming is referred to several times in the Olivet Discourse. In chapter 24 of Matthew, it is mentioned in verses 27, 30, 37, 39, 42, and 44. In chapter 25 of Matthew, it is mentioned in verses 13 and 31. The most prominent reference to the second coming is in Matthew 24:30 (NASB): "And then the sign of the Son of Man will appear in the sky, and then all the tribes of the earth will mourn, and they will see the Son of Man coming on the clouds of the sky with power and great glory."

The "sign" mentioned in the verse quoted above is probably a large image of a crucifix in the sky. All the peoples of the earth will mourn for Him when they see the wounds suffered by Jesus in this image in the sky. Then they will see the second coming itself.

In the book of Mark, the second coming is mentioned in 13:26; 32–33. In the book of Luke, it is mentioned in 21:27; 34–35. It is also mentioned in several other places in the Gospels outside the Olivet Discourse, such as in Luke 12:40; 17:24; and 17:30.

References to the Rapture

As I discussed in the chapter titled "The Timing of the Rapture," I believe that the posttribulationist view is the correct view when considering when the rapture will take place. That is, I think that the rapture will happen at the same time as, or immediately after, the second coming. Consequently, I think that any reference to the rapture is inherently a reference to the second coming.

Therefore, I believe that the following three passages quoted from the New Testament, which prophecy scholars believe refer to the rapture, refer also to the second coming.

I already referred to 1 Thessalonians 4:16–17 when I discussed the timing of the rapture. Following is the entire six-verse passage that contains those verses.

> But we do not want you to be uninformed, brethren, about those who are asleep, that you may not grieve, as do the rest who have no hope. For if we believe that Jesus died and rose again, even so God will bring with Him those who have fallen asleep in Jesus. For this we say to you by the word of the Lord, that we who are alive, and remain until the coming of the Lord, shall not precede those who have fallen asleep. For the Lord Himself will descend from heaven with a shout, with the voice of the archangel, and with the trumpet of God; and the dead in Christ shall rise first. Then we who are alive and remain shall be caught up together with them in the clouds to meet the Lord in the air, and thus we shall always be with the Lord. Therefore comfort one another with these words. (1 Thessalonians 4:13–18 NASB)

Another reference to the rapture is in 1 Corinthians 15:51–53 (NASB): "Behold, I tell you a mystery; we shall not all sleep, but we shall all be changed, in a moment, in the twinkling of an eye, at the last trumpet; for the trumpet will sound, and the dead will be raised imperishable, and we shall be changed. For this perishable must put on the imperishable, and this mortal must put on immortality."

Last, but not least, consider John 14:1–3 (NASB), which was stated by Jesus himself. "Let not your heart be troubled; believe in God, believe also in Me. In My Father's house are many dwelling places; if it were not so, I would have told you; for I go to prepare a place for you. And if I go and prepare a place for you, I will come again, and receive you to Myself; that where I am, there you may be also."

Revelation's Chapter 19

Another reference to the second coming is in chapter 19 of Revelation, verses 11 through 16, and verse 21. Consider verse 11 (NASB): "And I saw heaven opened; and behold, a white horse, and He who sat upon it is called Faithful and True; and in righteousness He judges and wages war."

In this passage, Christ is portrayed as a horseman ready for battle, and the armies of heaven are following Him on white horses. (See verse 14.) Out of His mouth comes a sharp sword with which Jesus can smite the nations. Indeed, such is the fate of the armies on earth who have gathered to make war with Jesus. (See verse 21.)

Chapter 8

North vs. South

In chapters 10, 11, and 12 in the book of Daniel in the Old Testament, there is what appears to be a prophecy describing events that would take place between Daniel's time in the sixth century BC and the end of the age, i.e., the second coming of Jesus Christ. The events described seem to be in sequential order. Chapter 10 contains a description of how an angel of the Lord introduced himself to Daniel and explained to him that he had come to him in order to give him an understanding (a prophecy) of what would happen to his people in the end times. Chapters 11 and 12 contain the actual prophecy. Various points of this prophecy refer to the "king of the north" and the "king of the south."

Christian theologians, by and large, believe that verses 6 thru 35 in chapter 11 are describing the activities of the leader of the Seleucid empire based in Syria (the king of the north) and the leader of the Ptolemy empire based in Egypt (the king of the south). These events are supposed to have happened in the second, third, and fourth centuries BC. The prophecy then jumps over two thousand years to the time of the Antichrist, a description of whom starts in verse 36. The rest of chapter 11 and chapter 12, describe what will happen from the time of the Antichrist up until the time of the second coming.

However, there are a couple of flaws in the theory that verses 6 through 35 describe the Seleucid and Ptolemy empires. The more prominent flaw is seen by reading verse 11:13 (NASB): "For the king of the North will again raise a greater multitude than the former, and after an interval of some years he will press on with a great army and much equipment."

A footnote in my NASB reveals that the literal translation of the Hebrew expression translated "after an interval of some years" is actually "at the end of the times, years." In several places in the book of Daniel, the word *time* actually means "year." That appears to be the case here. So, verse 13 is probably referring to activity in the twentieth century when European powers took control of much land in the Middle East. If verse 13 is referring to activity in the twentieth century, then all of the verses following verse 13 in chapter 11 (and also chapter 12) are referring to activity in the twentieth and twenty-first centuries rather than Seleucid and Ptolemy activity in the second and third centuries BC.

Another flaw appears to be the abrupt manner in which chapter 11 supposedly describes the activities of the Seleucid and Ptolemy empires up through verse 35. In verse 36, it suddenly jumps ahead more than two thousand years to the time of the Antichrist. In five other verses in chapter 11 (verses 6, 7, 8, 10, and 13), a lapse of time is indicated. You would think, since there are several verses that indicate a lapse of time, that verse 36 would also indicate a lapse of time, especially since this is the largest lapse of time—more than two thousand years. But it doesn't. Therefore, verse 36 must not jump ahead two thousand years. Rather, verse 36 and the verses that follow it must be referring to the king described in the several verses before verse 36, possibly all the way back to verse 21.

Most prophecy scholars agree that verses 36 thru 40 describe the Antichrist. If so, then verse 35 and several verses before verse 35 must also be describing the activities of the Antichrist. In fact, it appears that the entire passage from verse 21 through verse 40 describes the activities of the same person, so a description of the activities of the Antichrist actually starts in verse 21.

Since it does not appear that verses 6 thru 35 in chapter 11 describe the Seleucid and Ptolemy empires, I have attempted to figure out which personages these verses actually refer to. The rest of this chapter describes the results of my analysis.

I start with the assumption that verses 21 through 40 describe the activities of the Antichrist. Then it remains for me to figure out who is being referred to in verses 6 through 20. I have also written a few things about verses 21 through 45 in chapter 11, and a few things about chapter 12.

First of all, the people referred to in verses 2 through 5—as agreed upon by most Christian theologians, with whom I agree—are as follows: In verse 2, the three Persian kings are probably Cyrus II (550–530 BC), Cambyses (529–522 BC), and Darius I Hystaspes (521–486 BC). The fourth king is either Xerxes I (486–465 BC) or Artaxerxes I (465–424 BC). The mighty king referred to in verses 3 and 4 is the Greek ruler Alexander the Great, who died in 323 BC. Following Alexander's death, his empire was divided among four of his generals: Cassander, ruling Macedonia; Lysimachus, ruling Thrace and Asia Minor; Ptolemy I, ruling Egypt, whose successors, the Ptolemies, ruled from 323 to 30 BC; and Seleucus, ruling Syria and the remainder of the Near East, whose successors, known as the Seleucidae, ruled until 65 BC.

The king of the south in verse 5 is Ptolemy I Soter (323–285 BC), and the strong commander was Seleucus I Nicator (312–281 BC).

Daniel's Chapter 11, Verses 6 through 20

Verse 6

Daniel 11:6 is probably referring to Cleopatra VII (as in "Antony and Cleopatra"), the famous Egyptian queen of the first century BC. The following discussion supports my view that verse 6 refers to Cleopatra.

Cleopatra became coruler of Egypt with her oldest brother when she was seventeen years old, which was when her father Ptolemy XI died. The "king of the north," which is mentioned in this verse (NASB), was probably the Roman emperor Julius Caesar, with whom Cleopatra had an affair, and by whom Cleopatra bore a son, Caesarion. But in 44 BC, Caesar was assassinated in Rome, and Cleopatra then returned from Rome to Alexandria in Egypt. The people "who brought her in will be given up." This expression probably refers to Cleopatra's supporters. The one who "supported her in those times" was probably the Roman ruler Antony, with whom Cleopatra had an affair after Caesar's death.

The fate of Cleopatra as expressed in verse 6 of the NASB was that "she will be given up." The NIV Bible says, "In those days she will be handed over." Legend has it that Cleopatra committed suicide by being bitten by a poisonous asp. However, neither of the two expressions above seem to express an act of suicide. So perhaps we should entertain the possibility that her death was an assassination. Several parties have entertained this possibility. According to Stephanie Dray, an author of historical fiction and fantasy, "it's become fashionable to challenge the manner in which Cleopatra died and also to suggest that she may have been murdered or forced to suicide."[1]

A likely suspect of such a murder is the Roman general Octavian, also known as Augustus. Octavian had conquered Antony and Cleopatra in battle. He was in control of Cleopatra's palace and had her imprisoned in her mausoleum. After he killed Cleopatra, he hunted down Cleopatra's fourteen-year-old son, Caesarion, and killed him. He probably did this because Caesarion, the son of Julius Caesar, was in line to be the next Roman emperor, and Octavian wanted to be the next Roman emperor. So, since Octavian had the motive to kill Caesarion, he also had the motive to kill the boy's mother, Cleopatra.

Near the end of verse 6, Cleopatra's father is listed among those who "will be given up" (NASB) or "will be handed over" (NIV). In a footnote in the NIV Bible, it is stated that the term translated as "father" can also be translated as "child." If the intended meaning is "child," then it is probably referring to Caesarion, not the two children Cleopatra bore by Antony.

Verse 6 indicates that the fate that befell Cleopatra also befell Antony. Yet legend has it that Antony was falsely informed that Cleopatra was dead and consequently thrust a sword into his breast. Later, another messenger came and informed him that she was still alive. Antony later died of his injury. So, just as it seems unlikely that Cleopatra committed suicide, it also seems unlikely that Antony committed suicide. One has to wonder if this also is a case where a homicide was passed off as a suicide.

Since the king of the north in verse 6 was a European (Julius Caesar), I assume that references to the king of the north in the verses following verse 6 are also referring to Europeans. I assume that references to the king of the south refer to leaders in the Middle East, most of whom are not Ptolemies.

Verses 7 and 8

Cleopatra was of Greek origin. The four smaller empires that Alexander's empire was split into were controlled by Greeks. Ptolemy I was of Greek origin, and Cleopatra was a fifth-generation descendent of Ptolemy I. In verse 7, the phrase "one of the descendants of her line" (NASB) is probably referring to another Egyptian of Greek origin descended from Ptolemy I. This person was probably a commander in the Islamic movement in the seventh century AD, which conquered the Middle East, northern Africa, and the Iberian Peninsula and made raids on other parts of southern Europe. Verses 7 and 8 are probably referring to this Islamic movement.

Verse 9

Verses 9 through 12 apparently describe the crusades between 1096 and 1270. Verse 9 refers to the first crusade, which was a French crusade. After these crusaders conquered some land in the Palestine area, most of them went home. The renewed spread of Islamic power in Asia Minor inspired the second crusade, which was led by Conrad III of Germany and Louis VII of France. It was so mismanaged that it accomplished nothing, and so it is not mentioned in these verses.

Verse 10

This verse must be referring to the third crusade. This crusade was in response to the taking of Jerusalem by the Muslim leader Saladin. The "multitude of great forces" (NASB) must refer to the expeditions from England (led by Richard the Lionhearted), Germany (led by Frederick Barbarossa), and France (led by Philip). Verse 10b (NASB) states, "One of them will keep on coming and overflow and pass through that he may again wage war up to his very fortress."

This must refer to the English force, since this is the only force that got as far as besieging Jerusalem. The German expedition collapsed when Barbarossa drowned in a mountain stream in Asia Minor on the way to the Holy Land. The English and French forces went to the Holy Land by sea. After they reached the Holy Land, they both besieged the city of Acre, which fell in July of 1191. The French force then returned to France. The English force was the only one remaining. It attempted to take Jerusalem from Saladin but was unable to do so.

Verse 11
This verse must refer to the fighting between the English force and Saladin's army at Jerusalem during the third crusade. The fourth crusade was strictly a European affair that did not involve the Holy Land, so it is not mentioned in these verses. There was no fighting in the fifth crusade, so it is not mentioned either. In the sixth crusade, Louis IX of France attempted unsuccessfully to take Egypt. The Holy Land was not involved, so this crusade is not mentioned.

In the second half of verse 11, the "great multitude" (NASB) that was raised was in the seventh crusade led by Louis IX of France and Prince Edward of England. This crusade failed. It was the last crusade.

Verse 12
The "tens of thousands" (NASB) who fell were the crusader forces that had settled in the Holy Land. By the close of the thirteenth century, the crusading Christians and the knights were ousted entirely from the Holy Land.

Verses 13 through 16
These verses refer in part to World War I (WWI), which lasted from 1914 to 1918. During the past several centuries, up until WWI, the Middle East and southeastern Europe were part of the Ottoman Turkish Empire. During WWI, the Ottoman Empire sided with Germany. Germany lost the war. Consequently, by the end of the war, the Ottoman Turks had lost their empire and retained only Asia Minor, which subsequently became the modern nation of Turkey.

Verse 13
The "greater multitude" (NASB) referred to in verse 13 refers to the great armies that the European countries had during the war. They were much larger than the "multitude" mentioned in verses 11 and 12, which were the European forces that participated in the seventh crusade. The second half of verse 13 (NASB) states that "he [referring to the king of the north] will press on [another translation is 'keep on coming'] with a great army and much equipment." Not only were there more military personnel in WWI, but the amount of equipment used was much greater than in previous wars.

The king of the north's act to "press on" or "keep on coming" began in the eighteenth century and culminated in WWI. These European armies encroached more and more on the land of the king of the south, i.e., the Ottoman empire. For example, by 1718 Austria had driven the Turks out of Hungary. Also, Russia annexed the Crimea in 1783. In 1821, Greece began its long fight for freedom. Russia waged war against the Turks again in 1806, and a third time in 1828–29, and won the Caucasus and the northern coast of the Black Sea. The Russo-Turkish war of 1877–78 brought Russia almost to Constantinople.

Also, by the end of the nineteenth century, the Ottoman Empire had lost Algeria and Tunisia to France and had lost Egypt to Britain. During WWI, a British army led by General Allenby defeated a Turkish army in Palestine and took control of Jerusalem and several other cities in Palestine. These losses, as well as losses in southeastern Europe and losses at the hands of the Arabs (verse 14), forced the Ottoman Empire to surrender on October 31, 1918.

Verse 14
Verse 14a (NASB) states, "Now in those times, many will rise up against the king of the south."

As it turns out, during WWI many Arabs in the Middle East did rise up against the authority of the Ottoman Empire. They were led by a British colonel, Thomas Edward Lawrence, better known as "Lawrence of Arabia." After a series of battles, his Arab forces completely destroyed the Fourth Turkish Army and captured Damascus.

Verse 14b states that some Jews would participate in this rebellion against the Ottoman Empire in order to bring to fruition the Old Testament prophecies about the Jews returning to their homeland in Palestine. But some of these Jews lost their lives in this rebellion and did not see these prophecies come to pass.

Verse 15
I have not yet figured out what World War I action is referred to in this verse.

Verse 16
The first half of this verse indicates that European armies could enter the Middle East at will and that the Ottoman Turks could not do much about it. The second half of verse 16 probably

refers to the British army led by General Allenby, which fought the Turks in Palestine as mentioned in the description of verse 13 above.

Verse 17
At the end of WWI, several treaties were signed, which ended the fighting between the Allied Powers and the Central Powers. One of them, called the Treaty of Versailles, ended the war between the Allied Powers and Germany. Also, the first part of this treaty drew up the constitution for the League of Nations, which was designed to abolish the likelihood of future wars.

The treaty that ended the fighting between the Allied Powers and the Ottoman Empire was the Treaty of Sevres, signed on August 10, 1920. According to this treaty, much of the former Ottoman Empire—including what are now Palestine, Iraq, Lebanon, Jordan, and part of Syria—was turned over to the allies to be administered by them as mandataries of the League of Nations. The first half of verse 17 is probably referring to the Treaty of Sevres.

Verse 18
The first sentence of this verse probably refers to the German leader Adolf Hitler and the conquests he made in World War II (WWII). The commander who put a stop to his scorn and repaid him for it was the American general Dwight Eisenhower, who was the leader of the Allied forces in the European theater of WWII. Such repayment was made by American and British bombers, which caused widespread destruction of German cities.

Verse 19
As Hitler was losing the war, he turned his attention to his Austrian and German homeland, away from the lands he had

conquered and then lost. When the Allied powers reached the German capital of Berlin, Hitler committed suicide.

Verse 20

The person mentioned in this verse hasn't appeared yet. It seems that we are currently living between the events of verse 19 and the events of verse 20. The person referred to in this verse might be a president of the European Union who will tax the member nations heavily in order to make the European Union a strong federal government over them. This person won't last long. Possibly, he'll be assassinated by supporters of the Antichrist, who is introduced in verse 21.

Daniel's Chapter 11, Verses 21 through 45

Verses 21–35: If, in fact, verses 21 through 35 describe the activities of the Antichrist, as I stated earlier, then we have fifteen additional verses we can study to learn more about what the Antichrist will be up to.

Verse 21: The Antichrist will come at a time of peace, rise to the top by political intrigue, and become leader of the European Union.

Verse 22: Maybe the "overflowing forces" that are "flooded away" and "shattered" (NASB terminology) are the military forces of the member states of the European Union. They may be incorporated into the European Union's military. The "prince of the covenant" (the chief Israeli temple priest in Jerusalem) being "shattered" may mean that this chief priest will lose his life. This may happen when the events in verse 31 take place. The chief priest—and possibly other priests and other Israelis—may lose their lives when they try to prevent the "abomination of desolation" from taking place.

Verse 23: The alliance mentioned in this verse might be the seven-year agreement referred to in Daniel 9:27.

Verse 24: In several places where the word *time* is used in the book of Daniel, it actually means "year." Verse 24 may be one of those places.

Verse 25: The Antichrist is the king of the north (Europe), and the king of the south is a strong Middle Eastern leader.

Verse 28: Possibly the plunder referred to in this verse includes oil concessions.

Verse 30: The first sentence in this verse is: "Ships of the western coast-lands will oppose him, and he will lose heart" (NIV). Perhaps "ships of the western coast-lands" refers to ships of the US Navy. In other words, the United States will come to the aid of the Middle Eastern countries when the Antichrist invades the Middle East a second time. Possibly the US government won't do this for the sake of the Middle East countries but to prevent the Antichrist from gaining control of Middle Eastern oil.

Verse 31: The "abomination of desolation" referred to in this verse, which is caused by forces of the Antichrist, is also referred to in verses 12:11 and 9:27.

Verse 33: Verse 33a (NASB) states, "And those who have insight among the people will give understanding to the many." In other words, people who realize that we are living in the end times, that the Antichrist is in power, and that the second coming is not far off (less than three and a half years at that point in time) will explain these things to the masses. Some of these knowledgeable people will lose their lives in the process.

Verse 34: The people who will join with them in "hypocrisy" (NASB) are Gentile people who will proclaim that we are living in the end times during the last three and a half years before the second coming, but they haven't really accepted Christ as their Savior.

Verse 35: Some of the people who have insight into what is going on will lose their lives in order to refine their souls.

Verses 36 through 39: These verses, of course, refer to the activities of the Antichrist.

Verses 40 through 45: These verses are discussed in the chapter titled "World War III."

If we are living in the end times and we witness the events in verses 20 through 35, then we will know that verses 6 through 35 are not referring to Seleucid and Ptolemy activities.

Daniel's Chapter 12

The prophecy in chapter 12, of course, is a continuation of the prophecy in chapter 11.

Verse 1: The time of distress mentioned in this verse is probably referring to the meteorite and asteroid/comet impacts, which will follow WWIII. The rescue of the people who are found written in the Book of Life is probably referring to the second coming and the rapture.

Verse 2: This verse jumps ahead one thousand years to the day of judgment, when almighty God decides who will go to heaven and who will be sentenced to the lake of fire.

Verse 4: The expression "many will go back and forth" (NASB) probably means that there will be much human activity between Daniel's time and the time of the end. The expression "knowledge will increase" (NASB) is referring to the vast knowledge mankind has gained in science, medicine, technology, mathematics, economics, and government since the time of Daniel.

Verses 5 and 6: The angel who was relating this prophecy to Daniel was joined by two other angels.

Verse 7: As I mentioned before, the word *time* in the book of Daniel sometimes means "year." That is the case in verse 7. "Time, times, and half a time" (NASB) means a year, two years, and half a year, or three and a half years. So, starting at the midpoint of the seven-year time period—that is, Daniel's seventieth week of years (Dan. 9:27; 11:31)—there will be three and a half years until "all these events will be completed."

Verses 11 and 12: The three and a half years mentioned in verse 7 is a period wherein one year has 360 days. So, this three and a half years has 1,260 days (360 X 3.5). However, verse 11 states that there will be 1,290 days, while verse 12 states that there will be 1,335 days. Two significant things will happen at the 1,290-day mark and the 1,335-day mark, but it is not clear which two things. However, it is possible that the second coming will happen on either the 1,290-day mark or the 1,335-day mark or on some day in between these two marks.

Chapter 9

The Eagle Has Landed

In 2 Esdras 11 and 12 in the Apocrypha, there is a description of a dream that the prophet Esdras had. (The Apocrypha is a group of books written during the time between the Old Testament and the New Testament in some Bibles. The prophet Esdras in the Apocrypha is the same person as the prophet Ezra in the Old Testament.) Chapter 11 describes the dream, and chapter 12 gives an interpretation of it, given to Esdras by an angel. The dream is about an eagle with three heads, twelve large wings, and eight small wings. In 2 Esdras 12:11, it is stated that the eagle represents the fourth empire in the book of Daniel. (See chapter 7 in Daniel.)

The purpose of this chapter is to analyze 2 Esdras 11 and 12 in order to gain insight about Daniel's fourth empire. I encourage the reader of this chapter to also read all of 2 Esdras, including chapters 11 and 12.

One thing that first comes to mind after reading chapters 11 and 12 is that this eagle might represent the United States, since the bald eagle was chosen in 1782 by the US Congress to be the emblem of the United States.[1] However, the eagle has also been chosen to be the emblem of several other countries and empires in centuries past, including ancient Sumeria, ancient

Assyria, the Roman Empire, Charlemagne's empire, Prussia, Napoleon's empire, the Byzantine Empire, Russia, and Austria.[2]

But 2 Esdras 12:11 states that the eagle represents the fourth empire in the book of Daniel, and the United States, by itself, is not the fourth empire. As will be seen in the following analysis, this eagle in 2 Esdras apparently represents European civilization, of which the United States is a part.

Chapter 12 states that the twelve large wings represent twelve kings or kingdoms who will rise to power in this empire one at a time, will govern for a while, and will then disappear. The eight small wings are stunted and represent eight kings whose rule will be brief and unimportant.

Many Bible prophecy scholars believe that Daniel's fourth kingdom, or empire, is the Roman empire. If it is, then the twenty wings of the eagle in 2 Esdras probably represent twenty Roman emperors, and the three heads represent three leaders who will come to power during the latter years. The large head in the center represents the Antichrist in a reborn Roman Empire.

However, as I discussed in the chapter "The Ten Kingdoms of the Antichrist," it is my view that Daniel's fourth empire is all of European civilization, rather than merely the Roman empire. The Roman empire is not the fourth empire. Rather, the Roman empire is the first dynasty of the fourth empire.

If the eagle represents European civilization, then it should be possible to figure out which twenty-three countries or empires are represented by the twenty wings and three heads. Following is an attempt to do that.

David L. Toney

First Large Wing on the Right Side

The first European empire to come to power after the demise of Alexander the Great's middle eastern empire (the third empire in Daniel) is clearly the Roman empire.

Second Large Wing on the Right Side

In AD 395, in order to ease the administration of the Roman empire, the Roman emperor Diocletian split the empire into two halves. The western half continued to be ruled from Rome. The eastern half was ruled from Constantinople. Each half had its own emperor. The western half was overrun by barbarians during the next century and ceased to exist. The eastern half continued to exist and became known as the Byzantine Empire.

After several centuries had passed, the Byzantine empire started to lose ground to the Ottoman Turks, who were invaders from the east. The Byzantine empire finally ceased to exist when the Turks conquered the Byzantine capital, Constantinople, in AD 1453. So the Byzantine empire existed for approximately one thousand years. Half of the amount of time that the Byzantine empire existed was approximately one thousand years divided by two, or five hundred years.

Verses 13 through 17 of chapter 11 state that each of the wings that would come to power after the first two large wings would not stay in power for very long. In fact, each of these wings would stay in power for less than half the amount of time that the second large wing on the right side was in power (500 years). The Byzantine empire satisfies this criteria for being the second large wing on the right, since all the succeeding European powers after the Byzantine empire have been in power for less than half the amount of time the Byzantine empire was in power. So, the second large wing on the right represented the Byzantine empire.

Note that this strong circumstantial evidence that the Byzantine empire was the second large wing on the right also supports the theory that Daniel's fourth empire is European civilization rather than just the Roman empire.

Verse 11:22 states that after a certain point in time, all twelve of the large wings and two of the small wings have disappeared. This means that all twelve large wings rose to power and disappeared before the third small wing rose to power. As I discuss later in this chapter, I believe that the third small wing to rise to power was Napoleon Bonaparte, who reached his high point during the years following 1807.

If this is true, then we have the starting and end points for a time period when ten of the large wings (from the third through the twelfth) rose to power and then disappeared. The starting point is 1453 (when the Byzantine empire ceased to exist), and the end point is 1807, after which Napoleon reached his high point. This time period is 1807 minus 1453, or 354 years long. During this time period, the third through the twelfth large wings rose to power and then disappeared, one after the other. Thus we have an upper limit (354 years) for how long any one of these ten large wings could stay in power. Three hundred fifty-four is less than five hundred. So the ten European powers, whichever ones they are, satisfy the criteria that each of them would stay in power for less than half the amount of time that the second large wing on the right side was in power (500 years).

Actually, if the entire 354-year period was spent on large wings rising to power and then disappearing in close succession, then the average amount of time that each large wing was in power (that is, for the third through the twelfth large wings) is

354 divided by 10, or 35.4 years. This time period of 35.4 years is much smaller than five hundred years (approximately half the amount of time that the second large wing, or Byzantine empire, was in power), which the reign of no subsequent large wing could surpass.

So, in our search for the European kings and kingdoms represented by the last ten large wings, we must search for kings and kingdoms that reign for about 35.4 years, not 354 years. If there were one or more lapses of time between the disappearance of any particular large wing and the next one rising to power, then the time period for these ten large wings would be even less than 354 years, and the average amount of time even less than 35.4 years. Calculating the average amount of time that a large wing used to rise to power and then disappear makes it easier to figure out which kings or kingdoms are the last ten wings, and the order in which they rose to power and disappeared.

Please note that in the interpretation of the dream given in 2 Esdras 12:4–34, the angel stated that the wings represented kings who would come to power at various times. The angel does not use the word *kingdoms*. Yet the reigns of the first two large wings on the right were each several centuries long. No king has ever lived for several centuries. So, whenever these first two large wings are mentioned, we should probably assume that they reference two *kingdoms* (the Roman empire and the Byzantine empire) rather than two *kings*. If this is true, then it may be that references to one or more of the other large wings are referring to kingdoms rather than kings.

Also note that one confusing thing about figuring out which large wings are which countries or which kings (for the last ten large wings) is the fact that when the European countries rose up and seized power, they tended to remain viable European powers instead of disappearing as 2 Esdras stated would happen. For example, the golden age of Portugal was in the early part of the sixteenth century. Yet Portugal did not become nonexistent later in the sixteenth century. Instead it has remained a European country right up until the present age. Evidently, Esdras meant that when a particular European country rose up and seized power, it was in a "golden age" of wealth, prestige, and economic and military power. What is meant by a country's "disappearance" is the fact that that country's "golden age" has come to an end, but the country continues to exist as a lesser power.

Verses 17 and 18 in chapter 12 state that after the second large wing ceased to exist, a great struggle for power would take place, and the empire (that is, the eagle) would be in danger of breaking up. This passage probably refers to the fact that after the Ottoman Turks defeated Constantinople, they kept pushing farther into Europe but were finally halted when they reached Vienna, Austria. They besieged Vienna but failed to capture this city. From then on, the Turks gradually lost ground to the Europeans until World War I, when they lost all of their remaining territory except Asia Minor. Asia Minor subsequently became the modern nation of Turkey.

Third Large Wing on the Right

Denmark's high point appears to have been during the fifteenth or sixteenth century. During this time, Denmark was a great Baltic power. An agreement called the Kalmar Union was the union of the three Scandinavian countries of Denmark, Sweden, and Norway and was formed in order to protect these three countries from other European powers. Denmark was the most powerful member of this union. So Denmark appears to have been the third large wing on the right.

Fourth Large Wing on the Right Side

Several large wings appear to have been European countries that engaged in exploration and colonization of the New World and parts of Asia and Africa, and who traded with those lands. The first one of these appears to have been Portugal, which apparently was the fourth large wing on the right.

The period of Portugal's greatness began late in the fifteenth century. Early in the sixteenth century, Portugal dominated Europe's trade with riches from its colonies, which included the part of South America that later became the nation of Brazil, and parts of the Far East. In 1580 the Portuguese royal family died out. The Portuguese throne was then claimed by King Philip II of Spain in 1581. So perhaps it can be said that Portugal's golden age disappeared in 1581.

Fifth Large Wing on the Right Side

Charles V, leader of the Holy Roman Empire, was the fifth large wing on the right. He became the most powerful ruler in Europe. During his reign in the middle of the sixteenth century, Spain (which was one of several European countries that were subordinate to him) became mistress of nearly half the world. (Note that the Holy Roman Empire, which existed throughout the Middle Ages, consisted mainly of the German states.)

Sixth Large Wing on the Right Side

The sixth large wing on the right appears to have been another colonial power, Spain. King Philip II became king of Spain in 1555, and Spain seized Portugal in 1580. Spain kept control of Portugal until 1640. Under the rule of Philip II, Catholic Spain attempted to conquer Protestant England, but the English defeat of the Spanish Armada in 1588 smashed Spain's rule of the seas. After the time of Philip II, Spain steadily declined in power and riches. So perhaps it can be said that Spain's golden age was in the middle of the sixteenth century after Charles V passed away.

First Large Wing on the Left Side

The next European power appears to have been the colonial power of England. The latter part of the long reign of Queen Elizabeth I, who ruled from 1558 to 1603, appears to have been England's golden age. The Renaissance reached England during this time, and it was a very prosperous period. The English navy defeated the Spanish Armada in 1588, establishing the superiority of English ships and sailors over all other European navies. English merchants found distant markets for their goods. Also, the most splendid period of English literature began in the latter years of Elizabeth's reign. When Elizabeth died at age seventy in 1603, English ships sailed in all the seas, and England was a wealthy and powerful nation.

Second Large Wing on the Left Side

Gustavus Adolphus, who lived from 1594 to 1632, is regarded as the greatest king that Sweden has ever had—and the best general of his time. Early in the seventeenth century, he took possession of the Russian territory along the eastern shores of the Baltic Sea. Later, he participated in the Thirty Years War on the side of the Protestants in Germany, where he was successful in several battles but was killed in the battle of Lutzen in 1632. Under his leadership, Sweden became one of the leading military powers in Europe. Sweden, during Adolphus' reign, is likely to have been the second large wing on the left.

Third Large Wing on the Left Side

The next European power appears to have been another colonial power: the Netherlands. The Netherlands declared themselves independent of Spain in 1581. In the first half of the seventeenth century, the Netherlands grew in wealth and power and had the largest merchant fleet in the world. They started to acquire rich colonies. So the first half of the seventeenth century was the golden age for the Netherlands.

Fourth Large Wing on the Left Side

The next large wing to come to power was the colonial power of France under the reign of Louis XIV, who ruled from 1643 to 1715. His was a powerful reign. Louis displayed much authority in France in the last half of the seventeenth century. Other European kings and queens were envious of the authority wielded by Louis XIV.

Fifth Large Wing on the Left Side

Peter the Great (1672–1725) was the greatest Russian czar in the Romanov family. He went to great lengths to "Europeanize" Russia. He went to war with Sweden and won much land in the Baltic Sea area. Czarist Russia under Peter the Great was probably the fifth large wing on the left.

Sixth Large Wing on the Left Side

Through his military genius, Frederick the Great, king of Prussia, transformed the German state of Prussia from a minor state to a first-class power, doubling its size in the process. Most of this warfare took place during the first half of Frederick's reign, from 1740 to approximately 1763.

The First Two Small Wings

Verse 11:3 states that the eight small wings are "rival" wings. Perhaps this means that they were rival to the large wings and the three heads. Verse 11:22 states that by a certain point in time, all twelve of the large wings and two of the small wings had disappeared. Verse 12:21 (NEB) describes the eight small wings' rise to power: "Two of them will come and go just before the middle of the period, four will be kept back until shortly before its end, and two will be left until the end itself."

I assume that the word *period* means the total period of time that the eagle would have, from the start of the Roman empire until the end of the rule of the last two small wings. If the second coming is going to take place a few years from now, which many prophecy enthusiasts believe, then the middle of this period must have been a little before AD 1000.

The First and Second Small Wings

There are two kings whose reigns were near the middle of the period and who stand out as likely candidates to be the first two small wings. They are Charlemagne (Charles the Great), a Frankish king who ruled from 768 to 814, and Otto the Great, a Saxon king who ruled from 936 to 973. Their short-lived empires existed only as long as these two monarchs lived. Charlemagne's empire included what is now France, Germany, Belgium, Holland, Austria, Switzerland, and the northern half of Italy. Otto's empire had roughly the same boundaries that Charlemagne's empire had. These two empires existed while the Byzantine Empire was in power. Thus, they were rivals to it.

David L. Toney

The Third and Fourth Small Wings

Verse 11:25 states that four of the remaining six small wings plotted to rise up and seize power. Verse 12:21 (quoted above) states that these four small wings rose up near the end of the period. During that time, the third and fourth small wings rose up to seize power, one after the other. According to verses 11:26 and 27, they both disappeared quickly. According to verse 27, the fourth small wing disappeared more quickly than the third small wing.

The two dictators who stand out as likely candidates for the third and fourth small wings are Napoleon Bonaparte and Adolph Hitler. For one thing, these two leaders disappeared quickly, and verses 11:26-27 state that the third and fourth small wings would do this. For another thing, verse 12:21 indicates that the third and fourth small wings would rule near the end of this period (or age), and if we are near the end of this age, it can be said that Napoleon and Hitler ruled near the end of this period. Also, Hitler disappeared more quickly than Napoleon did, and verse 27 states that the fourth small wing would disappear more quickly than the third small wing. Hitler's fast departure from the world stage, as compared to Napoleon's departure, is made apparent by examining the careers of these two dictators.

Napoleon came to power in France in 1802, when he became first consul in the French government. In a series of battles in 1805, 1806, and 1807, Napoleon brought most of Europe to his feet. The zenith of his power occurred between 1807 and 1812. From 1812 on, he lost power—first when he failed to conquer Russia in 1812, and also in 1813 when Great Britain, Austria, Russia, and Prussia joined forces and defeated the French. He attempted to regain his power in 1815 but lost the battle of Waterloo in June of 1815. He was subsequently imprisoned on the island of St. Helena until 1821, when he died of cancer. So, the time period during which Napoleon "disappeared" was from 1812 (when he was at his zenith of power) to 1821 (when he died of cancer)—a period of nine years.

Hitler came to the attention of other countries in 1933 when he was appointed chancellor of Germany. In 1934 the president of Germany died, and Hitler appointed himself president of Germany. He was then essentially a dictator over Germany. In 1939 World War II started when German forces invaded Poland. Germany conquered country after country and reached a high point of power in November of 1942. From then until 1945, Germany lost territory.

In May of 1945, Germany was finally defeated by allied forces, and it is thought that Hitler then committed suicide. The time period during which Hitler "disappeared" was from November 1942 (his zenith of power) to May 1945 (when he committed suicide)—a period of only two years and four months.

So, Napoleon and Hitler satisfy the criterion that the fourth small wing disappeared faster than the third small wing. (Two years and four months is less time than nine years.)

The Three Heads and the Fifth and Sixth Small Wings

After the third and fourth small wings disappeared, there were only the last four small wings and the three heads left. It seems likely that this is the period we are in at the present time. That is, the last four small wings and the three heads have yet to come to power. If this is true, then all of the remaining verses in 2 Esdras 11:28–46 describe events that will take place in the future.

In that case, we do not yet know who these last four small

wings will be. However, understanding who the three heads will be is another matter. Verses 11:28–31 state that two of these four small wings will plot to seize control of the empire. But then the middle head will wake up and, joined by the other two heads, will "devour" (NEB) these two small wings.

Verse 11:32 states that the middle head will establish an oppressive rule over the entire world. It seems likely, after reading verse 11:32, that the middle head will be the Antichrist, based in the European Union. The other two heads will probably be the second and third most powerful empires in the world at that time, which will probably be the United States and Russia. It also seems likely that these three heads are the same three kingdoms as the three horns in chapter 7 of Daniel.

It would be desirable to know which head will be the United States and which will be Russia. Perhaps we can figure this out by looking at verse 11:24. This verse states that two of the last six small wings moved away from the other wings and moved under the head on the right. (These two small wings will be the last two small wings to come to power.) What this probably means is that these two small wings are American political leaders descended from European people who migrated to America sometime during the last four centuries.

If this is the correct interpretation of verse 24, then we know that the United States will be the head on the right, and Russia will be the head on the left. Verse 11:33 states that the middle head will disappear, as most of the wings have done. Verse 12:26 states that the middle head, which is the largest, will die in bed. After this, the two remaining heads will obtain control of the world (verse 11:34). Verse 12:27 states that these other two heads will die in battle. Verse 11:35 states that the head on the right will "devour" (NEB) the head on the left. Verse 12:28 interprets this as meaning that one of them will defeat the other in battle. This will probably take place during World War III.

We know which one will die first. Verse 11:35 indicates that it will be the head on the left, which is Russia. And then the head on the right, which is the United States, will in turn be defeated (verse 12:28). As I stated in the section titled "2 Esdras Chapters 11 and 12" in the chapter titled "World War III," I believe that the United States will hit Russia with a preemptive first nuclear strike, thus defeating Russia. Russia, I suspect, won't have much of a retaliatory response, but it will have enough of one that the United States will also be defeated.

The Last Two Small Wings

Verses 11:37–46 describe how a lion will come out of the forest and accuse the eagle of doing terrible things to people throughout the world. Verse 12:32 states that this lion represents the Messiah (that is, Jesus Christ). Verse 12:2 states that the last two small wings will rise up to govern, but their rule will be very short. Verse 12:3 says that after they disappear, the eagle will burst into flames. What this may mean is that after all of the wings and heads have disappeared, the world will be struck by billions of meteors and meteorites and an asteroid or comet, which will cause worldwide destruction by fire. (See the chapter titled "Judgment from Heaven.") After this, the second coming of Jesus Christ, and the rapture, will take place.

Chapter 10

A Method of Calculating When the Second Coming Will Take Place

In chapters 9 and 10 of 2 Esdras in the Apocrypha, there is an interesting description of a vision that the prophet Esdras had in a dream. (The prophet Esdras in the Apocrypha is the same person as the prophet Ezra in the Old Testament.) The vision was about a woman who was in great distress, because after thirty years of marriage, she had given birth to a son who, after he grew up and got married, died on his wedding night.

In his vision, Esdras tried to console the woman, and while he was speaking to her, she suddenly changed into a city. After this, an angel explained the meaning of the vision. According to the angel, the woman represents the city of Jerusalem. The fact that the woman went through thirty years of marriage before giving birth to a son represents the fact that three thousand years passed before animal sacrifices were offered in Jerusalem. After those three thousand years, King Solomon embarked on his building campaign. He built the temple, his palace, and other buildings, and he started offering animal sacrifices. (See 2 Esdras 10:45–46.) The fact that the woman's son died on his wedding night represents the destruction of Jerusalem by the Babylonians. That was the end of the vision.

What initially puzzled me was this: what significant thing happened three thousand years before King Solomon built Jerusalem that could be used as a starting point from which to count out three thousand years? Solomon's building campaign took place in the tenth century BC. Three thousand years before that was approximately 4000 BC. It then occurred to me that the angel was referring to the passage of time since the creation of the world. In other words, time started when God created the world.

Some Christian theologians have attempted to figure out when the world was created by starting at the end of the Old Testament and counting backward. That is, they figured out when a certain king lived and reigned, and then figured out when his predecessor lived and reigned, and so forth, all the way back to the time of Adam and Eve. These theologians have generally agreed that Adam was created approximately 4000 BC, but they haven't agreed on an exact year.

Bishop Ussher is one of the better known such theologians. After his research, he concluded the world was created in 4004 BC. If we can figure out the exact date when King Solomon built the city of Jerusalem and started offering animal sacrifices in it, then we can calculate the year the world was created by calculating the date that is three thousand years *before* that date.

As I explained in the chapter titled "Evidence That We Are Living in the Latter Years," I believe that God created the earth 4.5 billion years ago, rather than six thousand years ago. I think that some other significant event happened about six thousand years ago, which can be used as a starting point from which three thousand years can be counted. What that significant event is, I don't know.

David L. Toney

According to 2 Esdras 10:45–46, after three thousand years, Solomon built the city of Jerusalem and started offering sacrifices. Of course, he did not build Jerusalem in a single year. It took Solomon several years to build that city, so we cannot pinpoint a certain year when Solomon built the city. However, perhaps we can pinpoint a specific year when Solomon started offering sacrifices in Jerusalem.

We know for a fact that he didn't start offering sacrifices at the Jerusalem temple until the day of dedication of that temple. On that day, he sacrificed several tens of thousands of animals at the Jerusalem temple. (See 1 Kings 8 in the Old Testament.) It seems likely that the day of dedication of the Jerusalem temple is the point in time when exactly three thousand years had passed.

So we need to figure out when this day of dedication was. We can calculate when the day of dedication was in relation to the beginning of Solomon's reign. However, there is a problem in figuring out when his reign started. Different sources pinpoint different years for the start of his reign. I checked six different sources for the start of Solomon's reign. The six dates I found are 960 BC, 960 BC, 961 BC, 970 BC, 971 BC, and 975 BC. These are six sources I checked:

On page 254 of volume 13 of the 1958 edition of *Compton's Pictured Encyclopedia* (published by F. E. Compton and Company in Chicago), the text states that Solomon became king about 960 BC.[1]

On page 154 of the book *These Were God's People* by William C. Martin (copyright 1966 by The Southwestern Company), the author states that Solomon's reign was circa 960–922 BC.[2]

On page 99 of the 1982 edition of the book *The Lands and Peoples of the Living Bible* by Bernard R. Youngman, published by Bell Publishing Company, the text states that the end of

David's reign (and therefore the beginning of Solomon's reign) was about 961 BC.[3]

On page xx (in the index) of the first edition of the book *History of the World* by J. M. Roberts, published by Alfred A. Knopf, Inc., the author states that Solomon reigned circa 975–934 BC.[4]

In its online article about King Solomon on the Internet, Wikipedia states that the conventional dates of Solomon's reign are circa 970–931 BC.[5]

On page 355 of the 1984 NIV edition of the *Oxford NIV Scofield Study Bible*, published by Oxford University Press, there is a large footnote that states that the united kingdom (all twelve tribes) was ruled by Saul, David, and Solomon, in that order, from 1050 to 931 BC. Verse 42 in 1 Kings 11 of this Bible states that Solomon reigned in Jerusalem over all of Israel for forty years. This means that Solomon became king in 971 BC.[6]

As I discussed in the chapter titled "Evidence That We Are Living in the Latter Years," there is a theory that there is a seven-thousand-year period of time set aside for mankind, and that the second coming of Jesus will take place at the end of the first six thousand years. Since the day of the dedication of the temple apparently took place three thousand years after the world was created (or after some other significant event took place), this day of dedication is in the middle of the six-thousand-year period. So, in addition to calculating when the world was created (or some other significant event took place), we can also calculate the exact year when the second coming will take place by calculating the date that is exactly three thousand years *after* the day of dedication.

Following is an attempt to make these calculations. I arbitrarily pick 960 BC for the year when Solomon started his reign, since, among the six sources for the start of Solomon's reign, 960 BC is the latest year and will therefore yield a year for Christ's return that is the farthest in the future. I don't want to mistakenly calculate a year that is closer than the actual year of His return.

According to 2 Chronicles 3:2, Solomon started constructing his temple on the second day in the second month in the fourth year of his reign. Assuming that his reign started in 960 BC, this was probably in 957 BC. According to 1 Kings 6:38, the temple was finished in the eleventh year of his reign. This was in 950 BC, and it took him seven years to build it.

After he completed the temple, Solomon spent thirteen years building his palace and other buildings. (See 1 Kings 7:1.) So, his building projects took a total of twenty years (1 Kings 9:10) and were completed in 937 BC. After the twenty years of construction, Solomon had a day of dedication of the temple. (See 1 Kings 8.) Many Israelis attended this dedication, and several tens of thousands of animals were sacrificed.

In order to calculate the exact year the six-thousand-year period started, we add three thousand to 937. Thus the exact year that the six-thousand-year period started was 3937 BC. In order to calculate the end year of the six-thousand-year period, the year the second coming will take place, we subtract 937 from three thousand to get AD 2063. We have to make a small correction by adding a year, since there is no 0 BC year (or AD 0). So the year is corrected to AD 2064. Thus, as of the year that I am writing this chapter (2014), we have to wait another fifty years before the second coming takes place.

However, another correction may be in order. According to some theologians, when prophecies concerning years are made, the years have 360 days each, instead of 365.2422 days each (the number of days in a solar year). For example, this is true of Daniel's seventy weeks of years. Thus the six-thousand-year period may have years with 360 days each, rather than years with 365.2422 days each. Assuming this is true, then in order to calculate the correct begin and end dates of the 6000-year time period, we make the following correction.

We need to calculate the number of solar years, which contain 365.2422 days in each year, that there are in a period of six thousand years of 360 days each. We can do this by solving a little algebra problem.

> Let x = the number of solar years in a period of 6,000 years of 360 days each.
> The total number of days in this period of 6,000 years can be expressed in two ways:
> 1) The total number of days = 360 (6000)
> 2) The total number of days = 365.2422x
> These two expressions are equal. So,
> 365.2422x = 360(6000)
> Solving for x, we have
> x = 360(6000)/365.2422 = 5914
> The number of solar years in a three-thousand-year period of 360 days each is half of 5914, or 2957.

So, the revised beginning year of the six-thousand-year period is 2957 + 937 = 3894 BC. The revised end date of the six-thousand-year period is 2957 - 937 + 1 = AD 2021. Thus, the second coming will take place in 2021. So, as of the year that I am writing this chapter, we have to wait another eight years before the second coming takes place.

This is a nice little calculation that I have made. However, there is just one problem with it. That problem is that it is probably incorrect. The reason I say this is that there does not appear to be enough time between now (2014) and 2021 for the Antichrist to come to power in Europe, and then for the seven-year international treaty to be signed and to last the full seven years, before the second coming. (Read the chapter titled "An Analysis of Daniel's Seventy Weeks of Years" to read about this seven-year treaty.)

Furthermore, before the Antichrist comes to power in Europe, there will be another strong leader of Europe for a short period of time. That leader has not come to power yet. (Read Daniel 11:20 and what I have to say about Daniel 11:20 in the chapter titled "North vs. South.") I would say that the second coming will probably take place sometime between 2024 and 2034.

I believe that my method for calculating when the second coming will occur is correct but that my input data—the year when Solomon became king (960 BC)—is incorrect. If I only knew when Solomon became king, then I think that I could accurately calculate the year when the second coming will take place. It wouldn't help to calculate using one of the other four dates I found, since it would result in a date for the second coming that would be even earlier than 2021.

It may be that the start of Solomon's reign was actually in 957 BC or perhaps 947 BC, in which case I calculate that the second coming will be in 2024 or 2034. We will have to wait and see when the Antichrist comes to power. When he signs the seven-year international treaty, then we will know that the second coming is only seven years away.

Chapter 11

An Analysis of Daniel's Seventy Weeks of Years

In chapter 9 of the book of Daniel is an account of the penance by the prophet Daniel during the first year of the reign of the Persian emperor Darius. This was during the time of the exile of the leadership of Judea to Babylon. In this penance, Daniel confessed the sins of his people, the Judeans, and stated that calamities had befallen Jerusalem and the Judeans because they had committed these sins. Then Daniel pleaded with God to forgive the sins of his people and to restore the fortunes of the Judeans.

While Daniel was praying, the angel Gabriel visited him. Gabriel told Daniel that he had come to give insight and understanding to Daniel. Gabriel then relayed to Daniel a prophecy about future events, a prophecy that is commonly called "Daniel's seventy weeks." The prophecy is given in Daniel 9:24–27.

The prophecy states that seventy weeks have been decreed for Daniel's people. Note that the word *week* used here is somewhat misleading. The Hebrew word that is translated in some Bibles as "week" actually means "seven" or "seven years."

Therefore, in order to make this chapter less confusing, I will use the phrase "weeks of years" instead of "weeks" to denote time periods of seven years each. Also in this chapter, I will show that the weeks of years are weeks of lunar years (with 360 days per year) rather than solar years (with 365.2422 days per year).

The First Sixty-Nine Weeks of Years

In the middle of Daniel 9:25, the angel Gabriel said, "From the issuing of a decree to restore and rebuild Jerusalem, until Messiah the Prince, there will be seven weeks [of years] and sixty-two weeks [of years]."

This turned out to be the case, as will be shown by the following analysis.

On page 335 of the book titled *These Were God's People* by William C. Martin (published by the Southwestern Company, copyright 1966), the author indicates that the Persian emperor Artaxerxes, in the twentieth year of his reign (445 BC), gave the Jew Nehemiah permission to rebuild Jerusalem.[1] Nehemiah was, in fact, appointed to be the governor of Judea. (Also see Nehemiah 2:1–10.) So, in 445 BC the seven weeks of years started. The period of sixty-two weeks of years apparently started exactly when the seven weeks of years ended, so a total of sixty-nine weeks of years passed until the arrival of "Messiah the Prince." This is verified as follows.

It is possible to calculate the year when the sixty-nine weeks of years ended. If we make that calculation, then it is possible to examine that stretch of history on or about the year the sixty-nine weeks of years ended, looking for a Jewish person who was, or later became, a world leader, and thus was likely to be "Messiah the Prince" (who was not only the Messiah for the Jewish people but was also the Lord and Savior for all ethnic groups throughout the world). Not only will we have discovered the identity of the Savior, but we will have verified that the sixty-two weeks of years immediately follow the seven weeks of years, with no gap in between.

In order to calculate the year when the sixty-nine weeks of years ended, we must subtract 483 years (7 X 69) from 445. Let us assume, for the moment, that the sixty-nine weeks of years are sixty-nine weeks of lunar years. Then, before we can do this subtraction, we must first convert the 483 lunar years into solar years. This is done by solving the following little algebra problem:

> Let x = the number of solar years that contain the same amount of time as 483 lunar years.
> The number of days contained in the 69 weeks of years can be expressed in two ways:
> 1) 360(483)
> 2) 365.2422x
> These two expressions are equal. So,
> 360(483) = 365.2422x
> Solving for x, we have
> x = 360(483)/365.2422 = 476 solar years.
> So, starting at 445 BC and advancing 476 solar years, we arrive at AD 32. Note that there is no 0 BC or AD 0, so 476 - 445 + 1 = 32.

The only Jewish world figure who was active in AD 32 who was likely to be "Messiah the Prince" was Jesus of Nazareth. The year AD 32 is the approximate time that Jesus rode into Jerusalem on a donkey and presented Himself as the Messiah and Savior. Thus we have here a strong piece of circumstantial evidence that Jesus of Nazareth is the Messiah and Savior. And we have strong evidence that the sixty-two weeks of years immediately follow the seven weeks of years. Verse 26 states that after the sixty-two weeks of years, the Messiah would be killed. This, in fact, happened to Jesus. So this is another piece of evidence that Jesus is the Messiah.

Some authors go a step further and attempt to calculate the exact days that the 476-year period starts and stops (March 14, 445 BC and April 6, AD 32, respectively).

Now, let us assume for the moment that the sixty-nine weeks of years are sixty-nine weeks of solar years. Then, starting at 445 BC and advancing 483 solar years, we arrive at AD 39. The year AD 39 is six or seven years after Christ was crucified and resurrected. It is not as accurate as the year AD 32 in answering the question of when Christ presented himself as the Messiah. Thus it is apparent that the sixty-nine weeks of years are sixty-nine weeks of lunar years.

Most prophecy scholars stop their analysis of the first sixty-nine weeks of years of Daniel's seventy weeks of years at this point. But there is one nagging question that remains to be answered. Why did the angel Gabriel refer to the sixty-nine weeks of years as seven weeks of years and sixty-two weeks of years? Why didn't he simply refer to this time period as sixty-nine weeks of years? Perhaps there was something significant that happened at the end of the seven weeks of years and the beginning of the sixty-two weeks of years. But what?

To answer this question, we must first calculate when the end of the seven weeks of years and the beginning of the sixty-two weeks of years took place. We can do that by converting the seven weeks of lunar years into solar years and subtracting the answer from the beginning of the seven-week period, which was 445 BC. To calculate the number of solar years in forty-nine lunar years (7 X 7), we must solve another little algebra problem.

Let y = the number of solar years that contain the same amount of time as 49 lunar years.
The total number of days in the 7-week period can be expressed in two ways:
1) 360(49)
2) 365.2422y
These two expressions are equal. So,
360(49) = 365.2422y
Solving for y, we have
y = 360(49)/365.2422 = 48 solar years.
Subtracting this answer from 445 BC, we have
445 – 48 = 397.

So we need to find something significant that happened in 397 BC.

At about the same time that Nehemiah was active in Jerusalem, the Jewish prophet Ezra was active in bringing his people back to God. Just as Nehemiah traveled from Babylon to Jerusalem to rebuild the city and walls of Jerusalem, Ezra led a large group of exiled Jews from Babylon back to Jerusalem and made efforts to bring the Jewish people back to God.

According to Ezra 7:7, this exodus took place in the seventh year of the reign of the Persian emperor Artaxerxes. The reign of Artaxerxes began in 465 BC, so this exodus supposedly took place in 465 – 7 = 458 BC. This date is not even near our date of interest, 397 BC. It would appear that Ezra's exodus to Jerusalem took place thirteen years before Nehemiah's trip to Jerusalem (458 BC versus 445 BC). So at first glance, it would appear that none of the activities of Ezra are significant events that took place in 397 BC.

However, some Christian scholars believe (for several different reasons that I won't go into here) that the activities of

Ezra actually took place ten or twenty years *after* the activities of Nehemiah rather than *before*. How can we resolve this apparent discrepancy between what the Bible states and what scholars believe? As it turns out, in the books of Nehemiah and Ezra, all of the references to Artaxerxes are without the "I," "II," or "III." In other words, there are no references to Artaxerxes I, Artaxerxes II, or Artaxerxes III. There are only references to Artaxerxes. So it would appear that in any reference to Artaxerxes, we don't know for sure which Artaxerxes is being referenced. (However, the assumption is made that it is always Artaxerxes I who is being referenced.) Actually, we can be pretty sure that in the book of Nehemiah, it is Artaxerxes I who is being referenced. This is because the twentieth year of the reign of Artaxerxes I (445 BC) fits so well as the start of the sixty-nine weeks of years.

But the references to Artaxerxes in the book of Ezra are another matter. Maybe if the references to Artaxerxes in Ezra are actually references to Artaxerxes II or Artaxerxes III, this would make Ezra come later than Nehemiah and would satisfy scholars' claims that Ezra's activities were later than Nehemiah's activities. As it turns out, Artaxerxes II started his reign in 404 BC. The seventh year of his reign was 404 - 7 = 397 BC. Thus it appears that we have found the significant event that took place in 397 BC, and it is Artaxerxes II who is being referenced in Ezra, rather than Artaxerxcs I.

In 397 BC, at the end of Daniel's seven weeks of years and the beginning of his sixty-two weeks of years, the prophet Ezra led many exiled Jewish people from Babylon back to Jerusalem—and also brought them back to God.

The Seventieth Week of Years

The middle of Daniel 9:26 states, "And the people of the prince who is to come will destroy the city and the sanctuary."

The city of Jerusalem and its sanctuary (temple) were, in fact, destroyed by the Roman empire years after the first advent of Jesus. It is thought by many prophecy teachers that "the prince who is to come" refers to the Antichrist. Thus it is thought that the Antichrist is descended from the peoples within the Roman empire. The Antichrist is currently "waiting in the wings" and will come to power within a few years.

Daniel 9:27 jumps ahead approximately two thousand years to the time of the Antichrist, approximately the present time. This is when the last week of years (the seventieth week of years) will occur. Verse 27 states that the Antichrist will make an agreement with many people for one week of years but that in the middle of this week of years (that is, after three and a half years), he will prohibit animal sacrifices and grain offerings. When the Antichrist first signs this agreement, he will probably be only the leader of Europe. By the time he prohibits animal sacrifices and grain offerings, he will have acquired control over some additional parts of the world, including Israel.

It is thought by some prophecy scholars that the agreement mentioned in verse 27 is the long-sought-after, final agreement between the Israelis and Palestinians. The signatories of this agreement will presumably include many other countries in addition to Israel and Palestine. Apparently, one of the stipulations of this agreement is the rebuilding of Jerusalem's ancient temple and the resumption of animal sacrifices and grain offerings at this temple. (This temple will have to be rebuilt if temple sacrifices and grain offerings are going to be prohibited by the Antichrist.)

By coincidence, the second coming will apparently take

place just a few weeks (of days) after the last day of the last week of years. Daniel 12:11 states that after the regular sacrifice is abolished, there will be 1,290 days. Daniel 9:27 states that sacrifices will be prohibited, starting in the middle of the last week of years (that is, after the first three and a half years). The last half of the last week of years is 1,260 days long (3.5 X 360 = 1,260). So time will continue to pass for at least thirty days after the last day of the last week of years (1290 - 1260 = 30 days).

But Daniel 12:12 indicates that time will continue to pass—at least until 1,335 days have passed. So there will actually be a total of seventy-five days after the last day of the last week of years (1335 - 1260 = 75 days). Presumably, the second coming will take place sometime within this seventy-five-day period. Once this agreement, or international treaty, has been signed, we will be able to calculate when the last day of the last week of years will be, and thus the beginning and end dates of the seventy-five-day time period.

Chapter 12

America in Bible Prophecy

Some Bible prophecy commentators are puzzled by the fact that, according to their view, America does not appear in Bible prophecy about the latter years. They figure that something bad will have taken place in America, which will render America no longer a viable power on the world stage during the latter years. Another view is that in the coming years, America will revert to the isolationism it experienced prior to World War II. However, I believe that I have found several passages in Bible prophecy that refer to the United States. Following is a discussion of those references.

Daniel 2 and 7

As I discussed in the two chapters titled "The Ten Kingdoms of the Antichrist" and "The Eagle Has Landed," I believe that the fourth beast (kingdom) in Daniel 7 is the European civilization (including lands colonized by European powers, such as America) rather than just the Roman empire. Thus the discussion about the fourth kingdom in Daniel 7 inherently includes a reference to America.

Furthermore, I believe that the ten horns mentioned in Daniel 7:7 are ten regions, or world powers, rather than ten

European countries, and that the United States is probably one of these ten horns. (See verses 7, 20, and 24.) Also, it seems likely that the United States is one of the three horns conquered by the large horn, the Antichrist. (See verse 8.) The other two horns are probably the European Union and Russia. Also, the reference to the ten toes on the statue described in Daniel 2 may refer to the same countries or regions in the Antichrist's empire as the ten horns discussed in chapter 7. If this is so, then the United States is one of the toes.

Revelation 17

The ten horns on the beast in Daniel 7 are also probably the same countries or regions as the ten horns on the beast discussed in Revelation 17. So, here also the prophecy inherently includes reference to America.

Daniel 11:18

As I discussed in the chapter titled " North vs. South," I believe that the prophecy contained in Daniel 11:6–20 refers to the interaction between Europe and the Middle East during the last two thousand years, and that the prophecy in Daniel 11:21–40 describes the career of the Antichrist. I think the commander referred to in verse 18 is the American general Dwight Eisenhower, who was the supreme commander of the Allied forces in the European theater of World War II. By referring to this American general, the prophecy in verse 18 is inherently referring to America.

Daniel 11:29

Daniel 11:29 is a reference to a second invasion of the Middle East by a European military force led by the Antichrist. Verse

30 states that this invasion force will be rebuffed by ships of Kittim. The word *Kittim* is translated as "the west." The only country or region west of Europe that is strong enough to put a stop to the European invasion force is the United States. So the word *Kittim* in this passage must refer to the United States. Thus we have here another reference to the United States in Bible prophecy. This attempted invasion of the Middle East will evidently occur after the Antichrist has obtained control of Europe but before he has obtained control of America. It will occur before the three-and-a-half-year period when the Antichrist will be able to do anything he wishes to do. (See Revelation 13:5.)

Jeremiah 50:41

Another apparent reference to the United States is in Jeremiah 50:41: "Behold, a people is coming from the north, and a great nation and many kings will be aroused from the remote parts of the earth."

The people coming from the north is either Europe or Russia, while the "great nation" must be the United States, since it is a great nation, and it is very remote from Babylonia (now the southern half of modern-day Iraq). Chapters 50 and 51 in Jeremiah describe how the nation of Babylonia will be punished because of the sins it committed against Israel. These sins were committed when the Babylonian empire conquered Judah, including Jerusalem, and forced many Jews to go into exile in Babylonia, several hundred years BC.

The punishment that God intends to mete out against the Babylonians still has not taken place. It will be a future event. (Operation Desert Storm was not this punishment, since it was not severe enough. Also, the recent war in Iraq is not that punishment.) In three other places in chapters 50 and 51, mention is made of a military force coming to Babylonia from the north. Besides Jeremiah 50:41, see also 50:3; 50:9; and 51:48.

Various verses also state that the resulting destruction will be so severe that Babylonia will never again be inhabited. For example, see Jeremiah 50:3, 13, 23, 39–40 and Jeremiah 51:26, 29, 37, 41, 43. We know that this invasion is a future event, because Babylonia has been continuously occupied ever since the time of Nebuchadnezzar. It has never yet been unoccupied.

It is not clear who the invaders from the north will be. One possibility is that they will be the European Union, who may be provoked into attacking Iraq (or the Babylonian part of it) because a terrorist group based in Iraq has unleashed a weapon of mass destruction (a nuclear, biological, or chemical weapon) against one or more cities in Europe. In this situation, the United States would join the Europeans in their attempt to punish the terrorist group responsible for the attack.

Another possible reason for there to be an invasion from the European Union (where the Antichrist will be based) is that the Iraqis may refuse to kowtow to the Antichrist. In this situation, the United States would either join the Europeans or oppose them, depending on whether or not the Antichrist had obtained control of the United States at that point.

Another possibility is that the invading force will be from Russia, which may invade more of the Middle East than just Israel (as described in Ezekiel 38 and 39). When the Antichrist begins to lose control over the world after his three and a half years of unlimited power have ended, then Russia may be tempted to invade Iraq to capture its oil fields and/or to obtain a warm-water port in southern Iraq, which Russia has always wanted. Or Russia may simply wish to expand its empire. In any one of these situations, the United States would oppose the Russian invasion.

Ezekiel 38 and 39

At first glance, there does not appear to be a reference to America in Ezekiel 38 and 39. However, another inherent reference to America may be in the first line of Ezekiel 38:6: "Gomer with all its troops." This is contained in a passage that lists the peoples who will participate in an invasion of Israel in the latter years. Gog, of the land of Magog, is portrayed as the leader of this invasion. He will lead Rosh, Meschech, and Tubal. They will be joined by Persia, Ethiopia, Put, Gomer, and Beth-Togarmah.

Gomer, who was a grandson of Noah, had three sons. They were Ashkenaz, Riphath, and Togarmah. Research reveals that Ashkenaz was the ancestor of the Germanic peoples. Tractate Yoma, in the Hebrew Talmud, states that Gomer is the ancestor of the Gomermians, who are modern Germans.[1] Some authorities have identified the children of Ashkenaz with the Scythians.[2] However, in Rabbinic literature, Ashkenaz is believed to be the ancestor of the Germanic people.[3]

Ever since the barbarian invasions that brought down the western half of the Roman empire, the Germanic peoples have occupied much of Europe. For example, the Anglo-Saxons who migrated from mainland Europe to England in the seventh century AD are Germanic. The Saxons migrated from northwestern Germany, and the Angles migrated from Scandinavia, which is populated with Germanic people. The Normans who migrated to England in 1066 from Normandy in France are also Germanic. (They originally came from Denmark.)

Modern English people are part Angle, part Saxon, part

Norman, and part Celtic (who are not Germanic.) Some Anglo-Saxons also settled in Ireland, Scotland, and Wales, and some Scandinavian people settled in Scotland. Also, the Franks and Visigoths who settled in France are Germanic. (Some Celtic people, who are not Germanic, also live in France.) Some Visigoths settled in Spain. Some Ostrogoths settled in the Black Sea region. (The Goths were Germanic.)

Also, some people of the German tribe, the Lombards, settled in a region in northern Italy, which later became known as Lombardy. Some people from Britain later settled in Australia. Thus, many of the English, French, German, Austrian, Swedish, Norwegian, Danish, Finnish, Dutch, Belgian, and Australian people, and a few of the Italian, Spanish, Irish, Scottish, and Welsh people are of Germanic origin.

Research also reveals that Riphath was the ancestor of the Celtic peoples. Gomer has been identified by some historians as the ancestor of the Galatians, Gauls, and Celts.[4] Some Irish traditions (and the Irish are predominately Celtic) say that Riphath is the ancestor of the Celts. The Celts occupied large parts of Europe before the time of Christ, including the British Isles, France (formerly known as Gaul), the low countries, much of central Europe, the Iberian Peninsula, northern Italy, and part of the Balkans. No doubt, many Celtic peoples remained in Europe after other peoples migrated into Europe. Many Europeans today are probably all or part Celtic.

Togarmah was the ancestor of the Hittites—Georgians, Armenians, and other peoples of the Caucasus—and the Turkic people.

Many of the North and South Americans who are descended from Europeans are, in turn, all or part Germanic and/or Celtic. Thus the phrase "Gomer with all its troops" may refer to several European countries and North and South

American countries. Also, notice that the word *all* is included in this phrase. This seems to imply that all of the above named countries or regions will participate in this invasion, including the United States. But even though they will participate in the invasion, they won't be led by Gog, who will be a Russian. They may, in fact, fight against the Russian invasion. (In order to fight the Russian invasion, they themselves will have to invade Israel.)

The reason for this Russian invasion is not clear. Chapter 38 suggests that the reason is to gather plunder. Yet there doesn't seem to be much to plunder in Israel. Some commentators have suggested that the reason is a deep-seated anti-Semitism in Russia. But it doesn't seem likely that Russia would go to the bother of invading Israel because of such hatred.

Another possible reason has occurred to me. When the Antichrist has acquired control of the world, he may move his headquarters to Jerusalem, where he can display himself as God in the Israeli temple. After moving to Jerusalem, he may accumulate many riches there. For example, he may dictate to all the countries of the world that they must move their gold reserves to his headquarters in Jerusalem.

After the Antichrist's three-and-a-half-year period of unlimited power has expired, some countries in his former empire might be tempted to rebel against his authority. So a desire to acquire all the gold in the world might be one reason for the Russian invasion. The European Union and the United States would not stand for such an invasion, since they would want to get back their share of the gold. So they too would invade Israel in order to fight the Russians.

David L. Toney

2 Esdras 11 and 12

More references to the United States in Bible prophecy about the latter years may be contained in 2 Esdras 11 and 12 in the Apocrypha. These two chapters describe a vision that the prophet Esdras had about an eagle with twelve large wings, eight small wings, and three heads. (Read the chapter titled "The Eagle Has Landed.") Second Esdras 12:11 states that the eagle represents the fourth kingdom in the book of Daniel. (See chapter 7 in Daniel.)

Since I believe that the fourth kingdom is the European civilization throughout the last two thousand years rather than just the Roman empire, I believe that the three heads represent three powers that will come into existence in the latter years. Specifically, I think that they will be the European Union led by the Antichrist (the large middle head), the United States (the head on the right), and Russia (the head on the left). The activities of these three heads are described in 2 Esdras 11:29–35; 12:1, 22–28.

Also, the two little wings that moved over to the head on the right, I believe, are two American leaders. (See 11:24.) Their movement away from the other little wings toward the head on the right is apparently meant to signify that, unlike the other six little wings (European leaders), these two little wings will be American leaders. These two little wings are referenced in 2 Esdras 11:24; 12:2, 29–30.

Please note that there is a lot of prophecy in chapters 11 and 12 and, in fact, throughout 2 Esdras. I think it is a mistake that 2 Esdras is being ignored by prophecy commentators.

Ezekiel 39:6

Last, but not least, anytime the word *coastlands* is mentioned in the Bible, it refers to all other lands and countries outside of Israel, including America. For example, see Ezekiel 39:6.

Chapter 13

The Last Seven Years Before the Second Coming of Jesus Christ

In this chapter, I present a summary of what I believe will take place during the last seven years before the second coming. This seven-year period is the seventieth week of years in the prophet Daniel's seventy weeks of years. (Read the chapter titled "An Analysis of Daniel's Seventy Weeks of Years.")

In this summary, I include the dates when I believe certain events will happen. All of these dates are relative to the day when the second coming will take place. In the chapter titled "A Method of Calculating When the Second Coming Will Take Place," I attempted to calculate when the second coming would happen. However, as I discussed in that chapter, I have probably failed to correctly make that calculation.

Consequently, since I don't feel confident that I know when the second coming will take place, I use the term "YEAR" in this summary to denote the unknown year when it will take place. The year of a certain event that takes place shortly before the second coming is denoted by "YEAR minus a few years."

For example, according to prophecy in the book of Daniel, the year when the famous treaty is signed, which allows the

Israelis to rebuild and use their ancient Jerusalem temple, is seven years before the year of the second coming. Thus the year of the signing of this treaty is denoted as "YEAR − 7."

During Jesus' first advent, notable events of His life took place on Jewish holidays during the spring. For example, Jesus was crucified on Passover. So it seems likely that the second coming will also happen on a Jewish holiday. Two holidays that stand out as likely candidates because of their importance are the two holidays that make up the High Holy Days. They are Rosh Hashanah (the Jewish New Year) and Yom Kippur (the Day of Atonement), which follows Rosh Hashanah by nine days. These two holidays usually fall in either September or October.

In the following summary, I make the assumption that the second coming will be on either Rosh Hashanah or Yom Kippur (that is, in either September or October) of the year YEAR. Starting with that date, I have worked my way backward to calculate when certain events will take place, relative to the date of the second coming. The results are as follows:

YEAR − 9: The predecessor of the Antichrist in Europe will become president of the European Union. He will levy taxes against the member nations in this union and will make the European Union government a strong federal government over them. (See Daniel 11:20 in the Old Testament.)

YEAR − 8: The Antichrist will succeed the leader mentioned above. (See Daniel 11:21.)

August, YEAR − 7: The Antichrist, as leader of Europe, will make a seven-year agreement or alliance with several countries outside of Europe. These countries will include the United States, Russia, Israel, several Muslim countries in the Middle

East, and possibly several other countries. As I mentioned above, this seven-year agreement is the last week in Daniel's seventy weeks, where one week is a period of seven years of 360 days each. (Read Daniel 9:24–27). It may also be, or include, the long-sought-after agreement after the so-called "final status" talks have taken place between Israel and the Palestinians.

The Persian emperor Artaxerxes I allowed the Jewish leader Nehemiah to return from Babylonian exile to the ruins of Jerusalem at the beginning of the seven-week period in Daniel's seventy weeks in 445 BC. He was allowed to rebuild Jerusalem and establish Judah as a valid nation within the Persian empire. Also, Artaxerxes II allowed the Jewish prophet Ezra to return to Jerusalem in 397 BC at the beginning of the sixty-two-week period to persuade the Jews there to rekindle their faith in God, obey His laws, and carry out the rituals at the Jerusalem temple in the manner that was prescribed for them several centuries earlier.

Likewise, this twenty-first-century agreement (the seventieth week of years) will legitimize the modern nation-state of Israel as a valid nation in the world community and will permit the Israelis to rebuild their ancient temple in Jerusalem and to perform the animal sacrifices and other rituals at this newly built temple that were prescribed for them by God almost three thousand years earlier.

The temple will be built at its original site on the Temple Mount in the old city of Jerusalem, north of the Dome of the Rock. The two current Muslim structures, the Dome of the Rock in the middle of the Temple Mount and the mosque at the south end of the Temple Mount, will remain undisturbed. (See Revelation 11:1–2 and Daniel 9:24–27.)

At some point during these seven years, two witnesses will arise and prophesy about things that are going to happen during the next few years. They will prophesy for 1,260 days (three and a half years of 360 days each). The Antichrist will then take their lives. For three and a half days, their bodies will lie in the street, viewed by people in every nation. This may be done by one or more television networks televising an image of their bodies. They will then be called up to heaven (both body and soul)—to the astonishment of people throughout the world.

It is not known when the exact beginning and ending dates of their 1,260-day period of prophecy will be in relation to other things that will happen in the latter years, but it seems likely that the end point will be sometime before World War III (WWIII) starts, while the Antichrist is still in power. (See Revelation 11.)

August, YEAR - 7 through July, YEAR - 6: For a period of one "time" (year), the Antichrist will gain additional power through political intrigue and will distribute possessions and top political appointments to his top followers. (See Daniel 11:24.)

August, YEAR - 6 through January, YEAR - 5: The Antichrist, as leader of the European Union, will abandon his strategy of peace and will mount a successful military campaign against the Middle East. He will have a face-to-face meeting with the Muslim leader of the Middle East, and he will gain much plunder, possibly including oil concessions from the Persian Gulf nations. (See Daniel 11:25–28.)

February, YEAR - 5 through May, YEAR - 5: The Antichrist, not content with the plunder he received as a result of his first military campaign, will mount a second military campaign against the Middle East, but he will be stopped by the US Navy. (See Daniel 11:29–30.) In the *New International Version* of the

Bible, "ships of the western coast-lands" must be the US Navy, since the US Navy is the only western navy—west of Europe—capable of stopping this invasion by the Antichrist. The term *Kittim*—or *Chittim* in other Bibles—should be translated as "western coastlands."

June, YEAR - 5: In this month, the three-and-a-half-year period begins, during which the Antichrist, with Satan's assistance, will execute his authority. (See Revelation 13:5 and Daniel 7:25.) During the first year or two of this three-and-a-half-year period, the Antichrist will, by political intrigue, acquire control over the United States and Russia, which, together with the European Union, constitute the three horns mentioned in Daniel 7:8 and the three eagle's heads described in 2 Esdras 11 and 12 in the Apocrypha. Then he will acquire control over the rest of the world. (See Revelation 13:7; Daniel 7:24; and Revelation 17:12–13.)

February, YEAR - 3: This is the midpoint of the seven-year period. Forces from the Antichrist will stop the ritual animal sacrifices at the Israeli temple in Jerusalem and will cause the abomination of desolation. (See Daniel 9:27; 11:31; 8:11; 12:11.)

Revelation 12:6 indicates that the Israelis will find refuge in the latter years for a period of 1,260 days (which is three and a half years of 360 days each). The exact beginning and ending points are not indicated, but it seems likely that this time period will coincide approximately with the last half of the seven-year period because of all the terrible things that are going to happen then. The exact place of refuge is not given. The Israelis might literally "take to the hills" in the Israel/Palestine area, or they might find refuge in other nations.

Sometime during the last year or two of this seven-year period, strange locust-like insects with the sting of scorpions will be released upon the earth. Their sting will cause people who are stung by them to have much pain for a period of five months. Possibly, these insects are being, or will be, created in a military laboratory somewhere in the world by genetic engineering performed on an existing species of insect. Their release from the laboratory may be by accident—or it may be on purpose if it happens during WWIII. (See Revelation 9.)

February, YEAR - 3 through December, YEAR - 2: During this time period, the evil Antichrist will enter the Jerusalem temple and demand that he be worshiped as God by everybody in the world. Everybody will be required to signify their acceptance of him as God by having his mark—either his name or the number of his name, which is 666—on his or her forehead or right hand. Most people will accept his mark, but the saints (saved people) will refuse to worship him and will refuse to accept his mark. Some, but not all, of the saints will be either martyred or imprisoned for refusing it. (See 2 Thessalonians 2:1–4 and Revelation 13.)

The Antichrist will have an assistant who will be a false prophet and will work on his behalf. Also, an image of the Antichrist will be made, which will have human-like powers. It may be that this image will be a clone of the Antichrist. If it is, and the second coming occurs sometime in the next twenty years, then a woman must have given birth to this clone several years before the writing of this book in order to give it time to grow up and become a man. (See Revelation 13.)

December, YEAR - 2 : This is the end point of the three-and-a-half-year period of authority for the Antichrist. Very soon after this point, the Antichrist's worldwide dictatorship will begin to fall apart, and WWIII will take place. Arab forces will attack the Antichrist's headquarters in Jerusalem (Dan.

11:40). This will be followed by a Russian invasion of the Middle East (Dan. 11:40; Ezek. 38, 39). Escalating conventional warfare among many countries will lead to worldwide nuclear warfare (Rev. 9:15–19; Zech. 14:12). In this warfare, the United States will defeat Russia but will sustain some damage. See the chapter titled "World War III."

March, YEAR – 1: Two American leaders will briefly attempt to establish control over this heavily damaged fourth empire of Daniel. The fourth empire is the European civilization, which started with the Roman empire and includes not only Europe but also lands the Europeans have conquered and settled in, such as America. (See Daniel 7 and 2 Esdras 11:33–35; 12:2 in the Apocrypha.) Although the Antichrist will lose his worldwide empire, he'll remain alive until the second coming takes place. (See 2 Thessalonians 2:8.)

June, YEAR – 1: The great bombardment of planet earth by numerous meteorites and an asteroid/comet will take place. Read the chapter titled "Judgment from Heaven."

April, YEAR: World War III and the meteorite and asteroid/comet impacts that the world will have suffered from will have done enough damage to cause central authority in each nation to be significantly diminished. Because of this, and because the three-and-a-half-year period of authority for the Antichrist has ended, Israelis who are faithful to God will be able to resume the temple rituals in Jerusalem, including the daily animal sacrifices. They will cleanse the temple area and resume such rituals 2,300 mornings and evenings (that is, 1,150 twenty-four-hour time periods) after they were stopped in the middle of the seven-year period. (See Daniel 8:9–14; 9:27.)

July, YEAR: This is the end of the seven-year time period. However, there will still be a few more weeks before the second coming takes place.

August, YEAR: As a prelude to the actual second coming, the sign of Jesus will appear in the sky and will be seen by everybody who is alive on earth at that time, and people in every nation will mourn for Him. The sign may be an image of a large crucifix in the sky. This may happen 1,290 days after the midpoint of the seven-year period (Matt. 24:30; Dan. 12:11).

September, YEAR: Sometime between the 1,290-day mark and the 1,335-day mark, the second coming of Jesus Christ will take place. (See Daniel 12:11–12.) While Christ is still in the air, He will send out His angels and cause the rapture to take place (Matt. 24:30–31). He will then go to Judah and save it. Then He will go to Jerusalem.

Many of the world's armies that have survived WWIII and the meteorite and asteroid/comet impacts will have congregated around Jerusalem. Jesus will set foot down on the Mount of Olives just east of the old city of Jerusalem. When He does so, there will be a large earthquake that will split the mountain into two halves, creating a valley in between. Many of the Israelis in Jerusalem will flee the destruction of the surrounding armies (Zech. 14:2–5). The surrounding armies will then be dispatched by the Lord (Zech. 14:13; Rev. 19:19–21).

October, YEAR: By the 1,335-day mark, Jesus will have defeated the surrounding armies, and this age will come to an end. (See Daniel 12:12.)

YEAR through YEAR + 1,000: Jesus will set up His worldwide kingdom and will rule over it for one thousand years

(Rev. 20:1–6). At the start of this thousand-year period, there will probably be a supernatural cleansing of earth's surface, atmosphere, oceans, and seas performed by the Holy Spirit in order to rid them of the pollutants caused by WWIII and the meteorite and asteroid/comet impacts to make the earth habitable again. Then, ten thousand of the raptured saints who were selected to be the first generation of this thousand-year period will inhabit the earth (Jude 14). These ten thousand people will probably consist of several hundred people from each of the earth's ethnic groups, which will be enough to eventually give rise to hundreds of millions of people in twenty-five to fifty generations in the thousand-year period.

YEAR + 1000 and beyond: After the thousand years, Satan will be released from his thousand-year prison and will tempt the nations into more warfare, but before the warfare starts, fire will come down out of heaven and destroy the armies that have surrounded the saints. After this will be the final judgment, when almighty God decides the fate of each person. Evildoers will be sentenced to the lake of fire, while the saints will inhabit a new earth and a new city of Jerusalem forever (Rev. 20:7–15; Rev. 21, 22).

NOTES

Chapter 1
1. Grant R. Jeffrey, *Armageddon: Appointment with Destiny* (Frontier Research Publications, 1988), 178.
2. Wikipedia, "Ussher Chronology." http://en.wikipedia.org/wiki/ussher_chronology (June 28, 2014).

Chapter 4
1. Hal Lindsey, *The Late Great Planet Earth* (Zondervan Publishing House, 1970), 52–54.
2. Ibid.
3. Ibid., 51.
4. Ibid., 57.

Chapter 5
1. Duncan Steel, PhD, *Rogue Asteroids and Doomsday Comets* (New York: John Wiley & Sons, Inc., 1995), 1.
2. Ibid., 39.

Chapter 6
1. *Strong's Exhaustive Concordance of the Bible* (Nashville: Thomas Nelson Publishers, 1979).

Chapter 7
1. Tim Lahaye and Ed Hindson, editors, *The Popular Encyclopedia of Bible Prophecy* (Eugene, Ore.: Harvest House Publishers, 2004), 349.
2. Ibid.
3. Ibid.

4   Ibid.
5   Ibid.
6   Ibid.

Chapter 8
1   Dray, Stephanie. "How Did Cleopatra Really Die?" www.stephaniedray.com/2010/07/05/how-did-cleopatra-really-die/. (Accessed June 28, 2014.)

Chapter 9
1   *Compton's Pictured Encyclopedia*, vol. 4 (Chicago: F. E. Compton & Company, 1958), 211.
2   Ibid.

Chapter 10
1   *Compton's Pictured Encyclopedia*, vol. 13 (Chicago: F. E. Compton & Company, 1958), 254.
2   William C. Martin, *These Were God's People* (Nashville: The Southwestern Company, 1966), 154.
3   Bernard R. Youngman, *The Lands and Peoples of the Living Bible* (New York: Bell Publishing Company, 1982), 99.
4   J. M. Roberts, *History of the World* (New York: Alfred A. Knopf, Inc., 1976), xx.
5   Wikipedia, "King Solomon." *www.wikipedia.com*.
6   *Oxford NIV Scofield Study Bible* (New York: Oxford University Press, 1984), 355.

Chapter 11
1   William C. Martin, *These Were God's People*, 335.

Chapter 12
1   Wikipedia, "Gomer." *www.wikipedia.com* (May 17, 2014).
2   Ibid.
3   Wikipedia, "Ashkenaz." *www.wikipedia.com* (May 17, 2014).
4   Wikipedia, "Gomer." *www.wikipedia.com* (May 17, 2014).